DISC

# GROLIER

# STUDENT
# ENCYCLOPEDIA

VOLUME 17

## VENUS

## ZOOLOGY

GROLIER

First published 2004 by Grolier,
an imprint of Scholastic Library Publishing,
Old Sherman Turnpike
Danbury, Connecticut 06816

Set ISBN 0-7172-5865-3
Volume ISBN 0-7172-5882-3

Library of Congress Cataloging-in-Publication Data
Grolier student encyclopedia.
        p. cm.
Includes indexes.
Summary: An encyclopedia of brief articles intended for use
by elementary school students.
 ISBN 0-7172-5865-3 (set: alk. paper)
 1. Children's encyclopedias and dictionaries. [1. Encyclopedias
and dictionaries.] I. Grolier Incorporated.
   AG5.G87 2003
   031—dc21                              2003042402

For information address the publisher:
Grolier, Scholastic Library Publishing,
Old Sherman Turnpike, Danbury, Connecticut 06816

Printed and bound in Thailand

**Designed and produced by The Brown Reference Group plc
for Scholastic Library Publishing**
Project Editor:         Sally MacEachern
Designers:              Stefan Morris, Colin Tilleyloughrey
Cover Designer:         Iain Stuart
Picture Researcher:     Sharon Southren
Editors:                Clive Carpenter, Tim Footman,
                        Shona Grimbly, Henry Russell,
                        Gillian Sutton, Matt Turner
Maps:                   Mark Walker
Illustration:           Darren Awuah
Index:                  Kay Ollerenshaw
Production Director:     Alastair Gourlay
Managing Editor:         Tim Cooke
Editorial Director:      Lindsey Lowe

# ABOUT THIS BOOK

The entries in this all-new 17-volume general encyclopedia are arranged alphabetically, letter by letter. So you'll find information on Alabama in Volume 1 and on Washington in Volume 17. Similarly, U.S. presidents, Canadian provinces, and countries of the world all get their own entries.

For instance, the entries on **Presidents, U.S.** (Volume 13, page 46) and the **United States of America** (Volume 16, page 43) list every president and every state, showing where you can find the specific articles about every individual president and state.

The article on **Countries of the World** (Volume 5, pages 13–14) lists every independent state in the world and gives its capital. The countries are grouped into continents, and cross-references direct you to continent entries and to those for individual countries. Population figures for the United States and Canada are based on the 2000 U.S. Census and the 2001 Canadian Census. Population figures for countries and cities outside the United States are based on mid-2000 estimates provided by the United Nations.

A special group of articles will help you with your school projects. They include book reports, debating, grammar, note taking, punctuation, research, and revision. In each case the entry gets you started and provides some helpful tips.

Each entry ends with a list of "**see also**" cross-references to other subjects in the set. They will enable you to find articles on closely related topics so you can read everything you are interested in—for instance, the slavery entry points to Abolition Movement; African Americans; Ancient Civilizations; Civil War; Confederacy; Douglass, Frederick; Emancipation Proclamation; Lincoln, Abraham; Tubman, Harriet; and United Nations.

There are two other cross-referencing devices that will also help you find information. The first are "**see**" references. They direct you from a term not used as an entry to the entry where the information will be found—for example, Rhinoceros see Mammal, Hoofed. The second are "**look in the index for**" references. They tell you that the set contains information about the topic and that you can find it by looking up the subject in the index. The index in every book covers all 17 volumes, so it will help you trace topics throughout the set.

Entries are illustrated with photographs, diagrams, timelines, and maps. The maps show the key geographical features, capitals, and major cities for continents, countries, states, and Canadian provinces.

Special boxes cover particular subjects in extra detail. **Key Facts** boxes give facts and figures about U.S. states, U.S. presidents, Canadian provinces, countries, and planets. **Did you know?** boxes provide detailed information about a wide range of topics. **Amazing Facts** boxes highlight fascinating or fun facts about the natural world and modern technology. **Biography** boxes introduce some of the most important architects, artists, inventors, musicians, scientists, and writers in human history.

# ✳ VENUS

**The closest planet to Earth, Venus can be seen before sunrise, when it is called the morning star, and after sunset, when it is called the evening star.**

The light that appears to be coming from Venus is really the light of the sun reflecting off the tops of the planet's clouds. Venus is always surrounded by a thick, dense layer of gleaming white clouds. The first space probes to fly through them revealed that they are made of carbon dioxide plus tiny droplets of sulfuric acid.

The clouds end about 30 miles (48km) above the surface of Venus. Strong winds blow the cloud layers around the planet. Moving at a speed of about 225 miles (362km) per hour, the clouds circle Venus in about four Earth days.

### Underneath the clouds

Venus has a dry, desertlike surface. More than 60 percent of it is covered with low-lying plains. Above the plains are two high, mountainous regions. Venus also has several large volcanic regions covered with hundreds of volcanoes, each over 12 miles (19km) in diameter, and tens of thousands of smaller volcanoes.

The atmosphere of Venus consists of about 97 percent carbon dioxide and 3 percent nitrogen, with small amounts of other gases. The atmosphere is densest near the surface of the planet, where the temperature is about 900°F (480°C).

Venus has the most circular orbit (path around the sun) of any planet in the solar system. It turns very slowly on its axis. A "day" on Venus is 243 Earth days. Venus rotates from east to west; most other planets revolve in the opposite direction.

Until the first space probes in the 1970s Venus was a mystery shrouded by dense layers of clouds. Although Earth and Venus are very different in many ways, scientists hope that by studying Venus they will add to their understanding of the Earth.

*Hundreds of radar images taken by the Magellan spacecraft in the early 1990s have been used to create a computer-simulated view of Venus.*

SEE ALSO:
Solar System;
Space Exploration

● **Look in the Index for:** ✳ **VERB**

# ✳ VERMONT

The state of Vermont lies in the northwest corner of New England. Its name comes from the French words meaning "green mountains."

Vermont is one of the smallest states both in population and in area. It is the only New England state that does not have a seacoast.

Vermont is divided into six geographic regions. The Green Mountains contain Vermont's highest peaks, Mount Mansfield, Camels Hump, Mount Ellen, and Bread Loaf. To the east are the New England Upland and the Northeast Highlands. To the west are the Taconic Mountains, the Champlain Valley, and the Valley of Vermont.

Vermont has more than 400 lakes and ponds, including Lake Champlain, a large expanse of fresh water in which people can swim, sail, and fish. Vermont's eastern boundary is formed by the Connecticut River.

In winter temperatures as low as −40°F (−40°C) are sometimes recorded. Occasionally, during the summer a heat wave will send temperatures above 90°F (32°C), but such extremes are rare and seldom last long. Vermont receives up to 40 in. (1,020mm) of rain and snow every year.

## Plant and animal life

About 76 percent of Vermont is forested. The most important commercial trees are sugar maple and white pine. In the 1800s so much land was cleared for farming that deer, beavers, wolves, and wildcats became rare. Now many species are returning. The catamount, or mountain lion, an important symbol of Vermont's wildlife, has reappeared. Deer hunting has become popular. Migrating geese and ducks gather in the marshes along Lake Champlain.

## People

Two-thirds of the population live in rural areas. Only one city, Burlington, has more than 30,000 people. For many years most inhabitants were New Englanders of English ancestry. During the 1800s immigrants from Ireland, Italy, Poland, Scandinavia, and Scotland arrived in large numbers. More recently immigrants from China, Vietnam,

*The state tree, the sugar maple, is the source of one of Vermont's tastiest food products, maple syrup.*

Mexico, and South America have moved to the state. There are also about 2,000 Abenakis, who trace their descent to the Native Americans who lived in the Vermont region before Europeans arrived.

## Economy

For most of its history Vermont was an agricultural state. In the late 1800s it became a major dairy producer, and today much of the milk used in neighboring states still comes from Vermont. Most Vermonters now work in service industries such as tourism and health care. Manufacturing of electronic equipment and furniture is also important. Food-processing factories turn Vermont milk into cheese, yogurt, and ice cream.

## History

The earliest inhabitants of what is now Vermont were the Abenakis. There were probably about 10,000 living in the area in 1609 when French explorer Samuel de Champlain reached the lake that now bears his name. In 1666 French settlers founded Fort Sainte Anne on Isle La Motte in Lake Champlain.

English settlers came from Connecticut and Massachusetts in the 1720s. During the 1750s the French and the English carried on a series of wars with each other. Each side had Native American allies. In 1763 Britain gained the region from the French.

Vermonters fought several important battles during the American Revolution. A band of soldiers led by Ethan Allen captured Fort Ticonderoga, on Lake Champlain, from the British in 1775. In the Battle of Bennington, fought in Vermont in 1777, American forces kept important military supplies from the British.

The opening of a canal network in the 1820s improved transportation and enabled Vermont's farmers to export their produce. During the Civil War (1861–65)

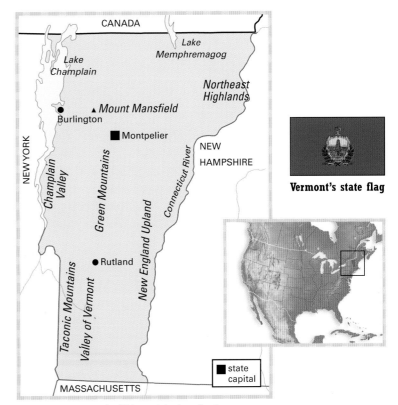

**Vermont's state flag**

the state sent half its able-bodied men to fight for the Union. They saw much heavy fighting, and casualties were high.

In 1900 Vermont was still mainly a farming state; but instead of raising sheep, farmers kept cows and produced dairy products. Increasing numbers of tourists visited Vermont during the 1900s, and skiing became popular in the 1930s.

Vermont's population has continued to grow, and now more than half come from another state. Since World War II (1939–45) Vermont has lost more than 75 percent of its farms. Its residents are trying to save farmland, and the state has strong laws to protect the environment. Many recent political debates have centered on how to maintain the state's rural character.

SEE ALSO: Civil War; French & Indian Wars; Revolution, American

*Look in the Index for:* ✴VESPUCCI, AMERIGO

# ✴ VICE PRESIDENTS, U.S.

If the president dies, resigns, or is impeached, the vice president takes over as president. If the president is disabled, the vice president becomes acting president.

**SEE ALSO:**
Constitution;
Government,
U.S.;
Presidents

Originally, the person who came second in the presidential election became vice president. In 1800 the Constitution was amended, and electors voted separately for the two posts. As a result, vice presidential candidates were often chosen for their appeal to voters in key states.

For many years the vice president had little power. Often the position remained empty when a vice president died or became president. It is only since World War I (1914–18) that the vice presidency has become as important as the Founders believed it should be.

## THE VICE PRESIDENTS OF THE UNITED STATES

Each vice president is followed by the president he served under and his dates of service. * means that he became president.

1. **John Adams*** (1735–1826)
   George Washington 1789–97
2. **Thomas Jefferson*** (1743–1826)
   John Adams 1797–1801
3. **Aaron Burr** (1756–1836)
   Thomas Jefferson 1801–05
4. **George Clinton** (1739–1812)
   Thomas Jefferson 1805–09
   James Madison 1809–13
5. **Elbridge Gerry** (1744–1814)
   James Madison 1813–14
6. **Daniel D. Tompkins** (1774–1825)
   James Monroe 1817–25
7. **John Caldwell Calhoun** (1782–1850)
   John Quincy Adams 1825–29
   Andrew Jackson 1829–32
8. **Martin Van Buren*** (1782–1862)
   Andrew Jackson 1833–37
9. **Richard Mentor Johnson** (1780–1850)
   Martin Van Buren 1837–41
10. **John Tyler*** (1790–1862)
    William Henry Harrison 1841
11. **George Mifflin Dallas** (1792–1864)
    James K. Polk 1845–49
12. **Millard Fillmore*** (1800–74)
    Zachary Taylor 1849–50
13. **William Rufus de Vane King** (1786–1853)
    Franklin Pierce 1853
14. **John Cabell Breckinridge** (1821–75)
    James Buchanan 1857–61
15. **Hannibal Hamlin** (1809–91)
    Abraham Lincoln 1861–65

16. **Andrew Johnson*** (1808–75)
    Abraham Lincoln 1865
17. **Schuyler Colfax** (1823–85)
    Ulysses S. Grant 1869–73
18. **Henry Wilson** (1812–75)
    Ulysses S. Grant 1873–75
19. **William Almon Wheeler** (1819–87)
    Rutherford B. Hayes 1877–81
20. **Chester Alan Arthur*** (1830–86)
    James A. Garfield 1881
21. **Thomas Andrews Hendricks** (1819–85)
    Grover Cleveland 1885
22. **Levi Parsons Morton** (1824–1920)
    Benjamin Harrison 1889–93
23. **Adlai Ewing Stevenson** (1835–1914)
    Grover Cleveland 1893–97
24. **Garret Augustus Hobart** (1844–99)
    William McKinley 1897–99
25. **Theodore Roosevelt*** (1858–1919)
    William McKinley 1901
26. **Charles Warren Fairbanks** (1852–1918)
    Theodore Roosevelt 1905–09
27. **James Schoolcraft Sherman** (1855–1912)
    William Howard Taft 1909–12
28. **Thomas Riley Marshall** (1854–1925)
    Woodrow Wilson 1913–21
29. **Calvin Coolidge*** (1872–1933)
    Warren G. Harding 1921–23
30. **Charles Gates Dawes** (1865–1951)
    Calvin Coolidge 1925–29
31. **Charles Curtis** (1860–1936)
    Herbert Hoover 1929–33

32. **John Nance Garner** (1868–1967)
    Franklin D. Roosevelt 1933–41
33. **Henry Agard Wallace** (1888–1965)
    Franklin D. Roosevelt 1941–45
34. **Harry S. Truman*** (1884–1972)
    Franklin D. Roosevelt 1945
35. **Alben William Barkley** (1877–1956)
    Harry S. Truman 1949–53
36. **Richard Milhous Nixon*** (1913–94)
    Dwight D. Eisenhower 1953–61
37. **Lyndon Baines Johnson*** (1908–73)
    John F. Kennedy 1961–63
38. **Hubert Horatio Humphrey, Jr.** (1911–78)
    Lyndon B. Johnson 1965–69
39. **Spiro Theodore Agnew** (1918–96)
    Richard M. Nixon 1969–73
40. **Gerald Rudolph Ford*** (1913– )
    Richard M. Nixon 1973–74
41. **Nelson Aldrich Rockefeller** (1908–79)
    Gerald R. Ford 1974–77
42. **Walter Frederick Mondale** (1928– )
    James E. (Jimmy) Carter 1977–81
43. **George Herbert Walker Bush*** (1924–)
    Ronald Reagan 1981–89
44. **James Danforth (Dan) Quayle** (1947– )
    George Bush 1989–93
45. **Albert Arnold (Al) Gore, Jr.** (1948– )
    William J. (Bill) Clinton 1993–2001
46. **Richard Bruce (Dick) Cheney** (1941– )
    George W. Bush 2001–

# ✳ VICTORIA, QUEEN (1819–1901)

**During the reign of Queen Victoria the British Empire reached the height of its power. Her strong sense of duty won her the devotion of her subjects.**

Victoria came to the throne in 1837, aged only 18, after the death of her uncle, William IV. At the time the British monarchy was unpopular with its people. The young Victoria was high-spirited and fun-loving, but her behavior was influenced by her marriage in 1840 to a distant cousin, Albert, a German prince. Albert taught Victoria that a queen should always act with dignity. They had a happy marriage, and by the time of Albert's death in 1861 they had raised nine children together. Victoria continued to maintain her interest in religion, morals, art, music, and fashion. Her reign is associated with a stern morality.

The prime ministers who served Victoria were men of great ability. They included Robert Peel, William Gladstone, and Benjamin Disraeli. In 1875 Britain gained control of the Suez Canal, Egypt, and in 1876 Victoria was proclaimed empress of India.

In 1897 Victoria celebrated her Diamond Jubilee—60 years of rule. People of all political beliefs showed her much affection. When she died four years later, she left behind an empire that seemed secure. Britain, however, would soon lose its place as leader of the world. Victoria was succeeded by her eldest son, who became Edward VII.

*This photo of Queen Victoria was taken in 1887, the fiftieth year of her reign. She reigned longer than any other British monarch.*

👀
SEE ALSO:
United Kingdom

# ✳ VIDEO RECORDING

**Video recording is the transfer of sight and sound images onto a magnetic tape (videotape) or onto a special kind of disk (videodisk).**

Video images can appear in several forms. The most common is still the video cassette. The earliest attempts at video recording were made in the 1940s. The Ampex corporation developed the first successful video tape technology in the 1950s. By the late 1970s VCRs (video cassette recorders) were widely available for home use. People could rent or buy prerecorded tapes of movies and other material. They could also record programs from the television. With a video camera they could make their own recordings of vacations, sports, business meetings, and other events.

From the 1980s various methods for putting video images on disks were marketed. Early videodisks could only hold two hours of information. They were also expensive. The DVD (digital versatile disk) has been more successful. Its picture quality is better, and a single disk can store more information. It is also possible to make home recordings on some forms of DVD.

Digital video images can also be stored on computers. They can then be transmitted over the Internet. New

*A boy holds a video camera. Videos can be used to record events such as the school play.*

technology includes a type of video recorder/player that can download images direct from a television without the need for tapes or disks.

Videotape is coated in particles that can be magnetized. Recording generates a magnetic field that corresponds to the signal coming from the television or from the image entering the camera. The particles arrange themselves in patterns similar to this field. When the tape is played back, electronics convert these patterns into a standard broadcast signal.

DVDs and other disk formats convert the data into digital form. The playback equipment converts a signal consisting of 1s and 0s into pictures and sound.

Video-recording technology is changing rapidly. Today's modern equipment may well be out-of-date in ten years time.

SEE ALSO: Computer; Internet; Magnetism; Movies; Sound Recording; Television

✳VIETNAM 👉 ✳ASIA, SOUTHEAST

# ✳ VIETNAM WAR
War devastated the Southeast Asian country of Vietnam between about 1957 and 1975. The United States fought on the side of South Vietnam.

*Helicopters fly over two American soldiers in 1967 during an attack in South Vietnam.*

France ruled Vietnam, then called Indochina, from the late 1800s. Between 1946 and 1954 the French fought a long and brutal war with the communist Vietminh, led by Ho Chi Minh. In 1954, after discussions in Geneva, Switzerland, Vietnam was divided at the 17th parallel. The Communists dominated the northern zone. The United States supported the president of the southern zone, Ngo Dinh Diem.

Communist guerrillas, called the Vietcong, began to attack the government of the south in 1957. U.S. troops secretly began to take part in the fighting. In 1963 and 1964 there were two military takeovers in the south. General Nguyen Khanh took power. The South Vietnamese government remained unstable during the war.

### America joins the war
In 1964 U.S. aircraft began bombing North Vietnam, and in March 1965 President Lyndon Johnson sent ground troops into South Vietnam. By 1969 there were 554,000 U.S. troops in South Vietnam.

In early 1968 the Communists launched the Tet Offensive, a series of attacks on cities in the south. They were not successful, but the attacks showed that in three years of fighting U.S. troops had not defeated the Vietcong.

Peace talks began in Paris, France, in May 1968, but with little success. The war was becoming increasingly unpopular in the United States, which was spending nearly $30 billion a year on the conflict.

Richard M. Nixon became president in 1969. He announced that U.S. troops would withdraw from Vietnam. The last U.S. troops left the country in 1972. A peace treaty was agreed on in 1973, but neither side kept to its terms. In 1975 forces from North Vietnam invaded, and the South Vietnamese government surrendered. Vietnam was united under communist rule in 1976.

More than 58,000 Americans died or disappeared in the war. More than a million Vietnamese also lost their lives.

SEE ALSO: Asia, Southeast; Johnson, Lyndon B.; Nixon, Richard M.

# ✳ VIKINGS
## Between the eighth and 11th centuries Scandinavian warriors traveled throughout Europe and sailed to Greenland and North America.

The Vikings originally lived in the lands that are now called Norway, Denmark, and Sweden. They were farmers and traders. They worshiped the Norse gods, including Odin and Thor. Their history and legends were recorded in long poems called sagas, which were not written down but passed by word of mouth from one generation to another. The Vikings were also expert sailors. By the late 700s they had built fast boats for war called longships or dragon-ships.

### Exploration and invasion
In the late 700s Vikings began to raid England, taking away many rich treasures and kidnapping people to sell as slaves. Over the next 250 years they carried out similar raids on England, Scotland, Ireland, France, and the Netherlands, and as far south as Spain and Italy.

However, they were not simply violent robbers. Swedish Vikings under Rurik traveled eastward from 862, and began a dynasty (ruling family) that would eventually become the nation of Russia.

*A fleet of Viking longships races across the North Sea toward England.*

When the Vikings invaded the northern English town of Eoforwic in 866, they renamed it Jorvik. Over the years this became "York." In 1664 English colonists changed the name of the Dutch settlement of New Amsterdam, naming it New York in honor of the English duke of York.

In 911 the Viking Hrolf, or Rollo, became the first Duke of Normandy, in northern France. Many of his followers settled in Normandy. Danish and Norwegian Vikings built settlements in northeastern England and in Ireland. The Danish King Canute ruled England between 1017 and 1035.

The Vikings also colonized Iceland. In 982 an Icelandic Viking named Eric the Red traveled farther west and settled in Greenland. His son, Leif Eriksson, explored even farther west and landed on the island now called Newfoundland, in Canada.

Christianity eventually replaced Viking beliefs and culture in Scandinavia and other areas of Viking influence. But Viking explorations and settlements had a lasting effect throughout Europe.

**SEE ALSO:** Exploration & Explorers; Scandinavia

# ✳ VIRGINIA

Virginia is on the East Coast. It was named in honor of Queen Elizabeth I of England, who was called the Virgin Queen because she was unmarried.

**Virginia's state flag**

Virginia is divided into five main regions. The Coastal Plain, called the Tidewater, makes up the eastern quarter of the state. Chesapeake Bay divides the Tidewater into the Eastern Shore and the mainland. The Eastern Shore is part of the Delmarva Peninsula, which includes parts of Delaware and Maryland. Major rivers flow southeast into Chesapeake Bay. Most of Virginia's northern border with Maryland is formed by the Potomac River.

The Piedmont is an area of gently rolling hills and rocky ledges. The Blue Ridge is a heavily forested mountain range. The Ridge and Valley region extends northeast from Roanoke. The Appalachian Plateau has many streams that flow in deep canyons.

Virginia has a moderate, pleasant climate. In the southeast winter temperatures rarely fall below 35°F (1°C) or rise in summer above 100°F (38°C). In the mountains the winter temperatures may fall to

**Map labels:**
state capital
MARYLAND
WEST VIRGINIA
DELAWARE
Shenandoah River
Washington, D.C.
Potomac River
Charlottesville
Chesapeake Bay
KENTUCKY
James River
Roanoke • Lynchburg
Richmond
Roanoke River
Newport News • Hampton
Norfolk
▲ Mount Rogers • Danville
Great Dismal Swamp
Virginia Beach
ATLANTIC OCEAN
TENNESSEE
NORTH CAROLINA

● **Look in the Index for:** ✳ VILLAGE

0°F (−18°C) and stay below 90°F (32°C) in the summer. Most areas of the state receive over 40 in. (1,000mm) of rain and snowfall each year.

## Plant and animal life
About 60 percent of Virginia is forested. Pines are found in the east, oaks mainly in the Piedmont, and hemlock, yellow poplar, black walnut, hickory, and maple in the west. Deer and bears live in the woods. Great Dismal Swamp is a haven for animals and rare plants.

## People
African Americans make up nearly 20 percent of the state's population. Large groups of people have English, Irish, and German ancestry. There are about 15,000 Native Americans. More than 70 percent of Virginians live in urban areas—cities, suburbs, and towns.

## Economy
Until the 1880s agriculture was the mainstay of the economy. Since then manufacturing has become important. Shipbuilding and the manufacture of transportation equipment are leading industries. Danville is the home of one of the world's largest textile mills. Chemicals and related products, including plastics and synthetic fibers, are important, as is food processing.

## History
When the English began to explore Virginia in the late 1500s, Native Americans had been living there for about 11,000 years. Some 30 different tribes in the Tidewater area belonged to a chiefdom called Powhatan, after its leader.

In 1607 the Virginia Company of London founded Jamestown, the first permanent English colony in America. Virginia's nickname, the Old Dominion, refers to its status as the first English colony.

Under the leadership of Captain John Smith, and with the help of Powhatan and his daughter Pocahontas, the colony survived. The tobacco trade became important. The first shipment of Virginia tobacco for sale in England was sent in 1614 by the colonist John Rolfe. In the same year he married Pocahontas.

By 1700 Virginia was the largest British colony in North America. White colonists relied on African slaves to grow plantation crops such as tobacco, rice, and sugar.

In the 1740s trouble developed both with Native Americans and with advancing French settlements, and the French and Indian War broke out in 1756. When the war ended in 1763, France gave up most of its claims in North America. The last battle between the colonists and the Native Americans was fought at Point Pleasant in 1774.

Virginia contributed many military leaders during the American Revolution, but combat in Virginia was limited to the final year of fighting, 1781. Four of the first five presidents were Virginians.

In 1831 a slave named Nat Turner led a revolt in Southampton County. Many whites were killed before he and most of his followers were captured and executed. As a result slave laws were made even harsher.

When Civil War broke out in 1861, the eastern counties joined the Confederacy, and Richmond became the Confederate capital. The western counties joined the Union in 1863 as the state of West Virginia. Virginia suffered greatly during and after the war. In 1870 it was allowed

*A male Powhatan painted between 1585 and 1593. Europeans gave the name "Powhatan" to all the Algonquian-speaking peoples who lived in the Tidewater area of Virginia.*

*Shenandoah Valley, Virginia, is an area of great natural beauty that attracts many tourists.*

to rejoin the Union and began rebuilding its industry to become one of the leading Southern states in economic terms.

Since the end of World War II (1939–45) Virginians have moved from the country to cities and changed from farming to work in industries and services.

SEE ALSO: Civil War; Colonial America; Confederacy; French & Indian Wars; Jefferson, Thomas; Madison, James; Pocahontas; Revolution, American; Slavery; Washington, George; West Virginia

*VISION see *SIGHT

# *VOLCANO

Melted rock and other hot substances inside the Earth sometimes erupt from beneath the surface. A place where this happens is called a volcano.

Heat in the Earth's interior continually escapes toward the surface. As it rises, it heats rock, which melts. This molten rock, called magma, usually cools within the Earth. Sometimes, however, the magma mixes with hot gases, such as steam. Gas-filled magma is lighter and can rise through a series of channels toward the surface. When it reaches a vent, or opening, in the surface, it spews out. Magma that comes out of a vent is called lava. During eruption it reaches temperatures of about 2,000°F (1,100°C). Cooled lava and other fragments build up to form the cone of a volcano. The hole at the top of the cone is called a crater.

Most volcanoes are located on the edges of continents. That is where the huge plates that form the Earth's crust rub against each other, creating faults.

**Types of volcano**
Volcanoes vary in height and shape. Volcanologists, the scientists who study volcanoes, divide them into four types.

Stratovolcanoes are formed from a number of layers of ash and lava. They usually have large, circular depressions at their summits. Mount Fuji, in Japan, is an example of a stratovolcano.

The largest examples are shield volcanoes. They form when large flows

Look in the Index for: *VIVALDI, ANTONIO

# AMAZING FACTS!

**About 90,000 people** died when Tambora, in modern Indonesia, erupted in 1815. About 10,000 were killed, and the others died of hunger and disease.

of lava spread out rapidly from central vents. Shield volcanoes have broad bases and gentle slopes. The large island of Hawaii is made of five overlapping shield volcanoes. The largest is Mauna Loa.

Small volcanoes, called cinder cones, dot the landscape in volcanic regions. There are more cinder cones than any other type of volcano. They form when small explosions of magma occur many times from one vent, leaving chunks of ash and lava on the surface.

The most powerful eruptions create ash-flow calderas. The magma and other material blow so far from the vent that there is almost no mountain. Instead, a wide crater, called a caldera, forms in a low hill of ash.

### Types of eruption

Scientists use special terms for the different kinds of eruption. The gentlest are Hawaiian eruptions, which are nonexplosive. Strombolian eruptions, named for a volcano in Italy, have many weak eruptions. Vulcanian eruptions produce a lot of ash but little lava.

Peléan eruptions are named after Mount Pelée, on the Caribbean island of Martinique. They are violently explosive, with rapid flows of ash, rock, and gases. The most violent eruptions are Plinian ones, which hurl plumes of ash many miles into the sky. They are named for Pliny the Elder, a Roman scholar killed when Vesuvius erupted in A.D. 79.

Scientists also classify volcanoes by how often they erupt. Extinct volcanoes

have not erupted for many thousands of years. Dormant volcanoes have also been inactive for many years, but might erupt at some time in the future. Active volcanoes can erupt at any time.

There are special observatories around the world where volcanologists can monitor active volcanoes. Earthquakes, emission of gases, and rises in temperature can be signs that a volcano is about to erupt. A violent eruption can kill many thousands, but with warning, people can be evacuated from the area.

▲
*Mount St. Helens volcano in Washington erupts. The massive explosion on May 18, 1980, created a cloud of gas and ash over 15 miles (24km) high. Scientists monitor the volcano for further eruptions.*

**SEE ALSO:** Earth; Earthquake; Geology

*VOTING see *ELECTION

## * WARFARE

As far back in history as we have evidence, humans have fought wars. Regardless of its rights and wrongs, warfare is an important human activity.

▲ *This mosaic is thought to show the Battle of Gaugamela in 331 B.C. The Greeks, led by Alexander the Great, won a great victory against the Persians, led by King Darius III (in the chariot). Alexander's army of foot soldiers armed with long spears and cavalry made up the finest fighting force of the age.*

Early peoples fought with clubs or bows and later with axes, spears, and swords. Hand-to-hand fighting was very tiring, and battles probably lasted only a few hours. An important part of early warfare was attacking enemy villages and building fortifications to defend them. Ever since, defending and attacking fortified places have been key parts of war.

Nomads (wandering peoples) in Central Asia started riding horses in about 3500 B.C. In about 1850 B.C. they built chariots, two-wheeled carts that served as stable fighting platforms. Chariots were eventually replaced by cavalry—skilled riders who charged at the enemy.

### Foot soldiers

Not every commander depended on cavalry. Although the ancient Greeks and Alexander the Great (356–323 B.C.) used cavalry, the core of their armies remained units of foot soldiers. The Roman army, the finest fighting force of its day, developed much larger units of foot soldiers called legions. Legionaries were foot soldiers armed with spears, javelins (throwing spears), and short swords. Superior tactics, discipline, and organization gave them an advantage even over a mounted enemy.

After the fall of the western Roman Empire in A.D. 476 cavalry dominated warfare in Europe and Asia. The cavalry armies of the Mongol Genghis Khan (about 1162–1227) conquered the largest empire the world has ever seen. In India armies fought each other mounted not only on horses but also on elephants.

By the mid-1300s in Europe English infantry armed with powerful longbows inflicted defeats on French cavalry. In the battles of Crécy (1346) and Agincourt (1415) English archers rained arrows down on heavily armored French knights, causing many casualties.

### Firearms

By then, however, a revolutionary new substance—gunpowder—had reached Europe from the East. Large cannons

Dutch and English ships fight against and destroy the Spanish Armada in 1588. This painting dates from 1608.

named siege guns helped Turkish forces capture Constantinople in 1453. The use of firearms spread swiftly. The 1600s and 1700s saw the rise of professional, uniformed infantry armed with musket and bayonet. Battles were very precisely planned and executed. Armies drew up in lines facing one another so that each man could use his musket.

New, lightweight cannons, named field guns, of the late 1700s arrived in time for the French Emperor Napoleon Bonaparte to make brilliant use of them. He broke with tradition, favoring flexible tactics and skirmishes, and concentrated his forces at the point where they would cause the most damage to the enemy.

By the time of the American Civil War (1861–65) firearms had developed to the point at which traditional tactics were no longer possible. Advancing lines of brightly uniformed troops would simply be cut down in a hail of gunshot. The need for infantry to seek cover and the arrival of railroads (a recent invention) greatly extended the scale of battles. Although Napoleon had been defeated in a day at Waterloo (1815), the Civil War battle of Gettysburg (1863) lasted three days.

At the front lines in World War I (1914–18) machine guns and artillery pinned troops in trenches and caused enormous casualties. Many soldiers died at Cambrai (1917), when tanks were first used on a large scale, at the gain of just a few miles of ground.

## Aircraft

World War I saw the arrival of two new weapons of war—the tank and aircraft. Tanks could roll over defensive trenches and were impervious to bullets. Aircraft were used to spy on enemy forces, to drop bombs, and to "dogfight" with enemy planes. Tanks and aircraft played an even more important part in World War II (1939–45), serving in every battle theater. Two atomic bombs dropped on Japan by U.S. airplanes in 1945 helped end the war—and heralded a new era.

## The atomic age

From 1945 to 1990 the United States and the Soviet Union, the victors of World War II, faced each other in a tense stand off known as the Cold War. Neither side dared attack the other because both had atomic and then nuclear weapons of enormous destructive power.

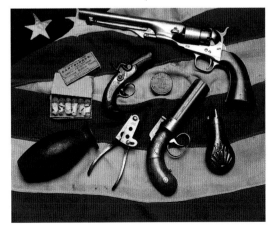

Revolvers with cartridges and gunpowder used in the Civil War (1861–65). The invention of guns changed the nature of warfare. It meant that soldiers had to seek cover, and battles lasted longer.

*A nuclear bomb can cause massive destruction and leaves a mushroom-shaped cloud in the sky. The explosion of the first nuclear bomb in 1945 changed the nature of warfare.*

## Modern warfare

Today's armed forces use guided missiles, satellite surveillance, and jet fighters. The line between war and peace is not always clear. In some countries there are civil wars. Terrorist organizations form "invisible" worldwide armies.

SEE ALSO: Aircraft; Air Force; Alexander the Great; Ancient Civilizations; Army; Balloon & Airship; Barton, Clara; Caesar, Julius; Civil War; Explosive; Hitler, Adolf; Knights & Chivalry; Korean War; Marine Corps; Mongols; Napoleon; Navy; Radar & Sonar; Revolution, American; Roman Empire; Ship & Boat; Spanish–American War; Vietnam War; World War I; World War II

# * WARHOL, ANDY (ABOUT 1930–87)

The American artist Andy Warhol was a leader in the style that came to be called pop art. He drew his subjects from American popular culture.

*As well as being an influential artist, Andy Warhol also inspired musicians.*

Warhol was born Andrew Warhola in Pittsburgh, Pennsylvania, the son of Czech immigrants. Warhol's exact birthdate is unknown, but he was probably born between 1928 and 1930. He studied art at the Carnegie Institute of Technology in Pittsburgh. After graduating in 1949, Warhol settled in New York City, where he became a successful commercial artist. By the 1960s he had won recognition as a painter.

Warhol's work aroused controversy at first because it disregarded traditional artistic standards. Among the images he depicted were consumer products, such as Coca-Cola bottles and Campbell's soup cans, and the faces of celebrities, such as the actress Marilyn Monroe and the Chinese leader Mao Zedong. Using a printmaking process called silk screening, he duplicated these images many times, varying only the colors.

Warhol became a celebrity. He was devoted to showmanship and art collecting. He also made experimental films, produced records, and wrote books such as *The Philosophy of Andy Warhol: From A to B and Back Again* (1975).

SEE ALSO: Art; Artists, American; Printing

* WAR OF 1812 [see] * UNITED STATES OF AMERICA

# ✳ WASHINGTON

**Washington is on the Pacific Rim, an area made up of all the lands that ring the Pacific. It is the only state named after a president—George Washington.**

Washington's landscape is varied and dramatic. The Cascade Range divides the state in two. West of the Cascades are beaches, rocky coasts, the majestic Olympic Mountains, the water maze of Puget Sound, glacier-fed rivers, and evergreen forests. To the east are arid deserts, a broad plateau and grasslands, rolling hills, and more evergreen forests.

The Columbia River carves a great arc across the state. Water is Washington's most valuable natural resource. It is used for agriculture, hydroelectric power, industry, fishing, and recreation.

West of the Cascades winters are mild, and summers are cool. Seattle has an average January temperature of 41°F (5°C) and a 66°F (19°C) July average. Washington's climate is drier in the east of the state. Rainfall ranges from 140 in. (3,500mm) to 16 in. (400mm). Some of the heaviest snowfalls in the nation have been recorded on Mount Rainier.

### Plant and animal life

Native Douglas firs grow in western Washington and can be hundreds of feet tall. Many more have been planted by the timber industry; they are harvested when they are about 60 years old. The salmon is one of the state's symbols. Animals include elk, black bears, deer, mountain goats, cougars, and coyotes. Wildfowl include ducks, grouse, and quail.

### People

Washington is growing rapidly, attracting people from other western states. The greatest number of people live in and around Seattle. In the 1990s most of the state's counties experienced population growth of between 10 and 25 percent.

The majority is of European ancestry. Asian Americans make up about 6 percent of the population, and African Americans more than 3 percent. Descendants of the state's first residents, the Native Americans, make up nearly 2 percent of the population. About half live on the state's 26 reservations.

*Wildflowers provide a carpet of color in Mount Rainier National Park. Behind them is the Tatoosh Mountain Range.*

**Washington's state flag**

## Economy

Washington's economy was long based on the produce of its forests, fields, and fisheries. Today the state's strong economy continues that tradition, but service industries and manufacturing have become increasingly important. Financial services, such as banking, insurance, and real estate, are especially important. Manufacturing industries produce aerospace and aircraft products. With its vast forests Washington is a leading state in the production of lumber, wood pulp, paper, and paper products. Microsoft's headquarters are based in the state.

*Two male elk fight. Many elk live on the slopes of the Cascade Mountains but have had their habitat destroyed in recent years.*

## History

People have lived on the land now called Washington for at least 11,000 years. Dozens of Native American groups lived in the area when European explorers arrived in the late 1700s. Bruno de Hezeta landed near Point Grenville and claimed the area for Spain in 1775. The Englishman James Cook explored the coast in 1778. He traded sea otter furs with Native Americans on Vancouver Island, and the fur trade soon brought English and American merchants to the area. Meriwether Lewis and William Clark entered Washington in 1805, traveling down the Columbia River to its mouth.

Spain gave up its claim on the area, and in 1818 Britain and America agreed to occupy it together. In 1846 the British agreed to accept the 49th degree of latitude as the boundary between their lands and the United States. In 1853 Congress created Washington Territory; before then the area was part of Oregon.

The railroad reached Puget Sound in the 1880s, and new towns sprang up along the railroad lines. In 1889 Washington became a state. Manufacturing became a major part of the economy during World War II (1939–45). Job opportunities and the natural beauty of the state continue to attract newcomers today.

**SEE ALSO:** Exploration & Explorers; Lewis & Clark Expedition; Pacific Rim; Washington, George; World War II

# ✴ WASHINGTON, D.C.
Washington, District of Columbia (D.C.), is the capital of the United States. The city was founded in 1791 to be the center of national government.

*The official residence of every president since John Adams, the White House is the oldest federal building in Washington, D.C.*

Washington is the center of an urban area that stretches into neighboring Maryland and Virginia. The Capitol building, on Capitol Hill, dominates the city skyline.

## History
In 1790 Congress decided that the new federal government should build its capital in a federal district—a place that was not part of any state.

George Washington chose the site on the Potomac River because it gave access to the sea but was far enough inland to be safe from foreign attack. The land was donated by Maryland. The original architect was Major Pierre Charles L'Enfant (1754–1825). The city was first named District of Columbia for the explorer Christopher Columbus. Congress later honored the first president by adding the name Washington.

## People
Much of the early city was built by free blacks and slaves. Today about 64 percent of Washingtonians are African American.

Washington is home to the Library of Congress, the National Gallery of Art, and the Smithsonian Institution, which is made up of 16 museums and galleries.

Professional sports teams include the Washington Redskins of the National Football League, the Washington Wizards of the National Basketball Association, and the Washington Capitals of the National Hockey League.

## Economy
Nearly 300,000 Washingtonians work for federal government agencies, of which there are nearly a hundred in the city. Washington is an international center for media. There are 14 television stations, 40 radio stations, and offices for almost every news agency in the world. It is the home of important magazines and newspapers, such as the *Washington Post*. Tourism is an important industry.

Washington has a subway system and three airports, including Dulles International. The main train station is Union Station, which opened on Capitol Hill in 1906.

## KEY FACTS

**AREA**
68 sq. mi.
(176 sq. km)

**CITY ESTABLISHED**
1791

**CLIMATE AVERAGES**
35°F (2°C) in January; 80°F (27°C) in July; 39 in. (990mm) rainfall a year

**POPULATION**
567,000 (total of 4.5 million in metropolitan area)

**SEE ALSO:** African Americans; Civil War; Columbus, Christopher; Government, U.S.; Library; Museum & Gallery; Segregation & Integration; United States of America; Washington, George

# *WASHINGTON, GEORGE (1732–99)

George Washington led the American forces in the American Revolution and became the first president of the United States from 1789 to 1797.

*George Washington's natural ability and personal integrity were key elements in the foundation of the United States.*

Washington was born on February 22, 1732. He had no formal schooling but was taught by tutors. In 1752 he inherited the family estate, Mount Vernon.

He served with courage in the French and Indian War. In 1759 he married a widow, Martha Dandridge Custis, and divided his time between his plantation and serving in the House of Burgesses, the Virginia state legislature.

In 1774 and 1775 Washington attended the Continental Congresses to discuss the colonies' plans for resistance to British rule. He was elected commander of the American forces and won important victories at Boston, Trenton, and Princeton. A number of British victories followed, but in 1781 the British were decisively defeated at Yorktown. The two sides signed the Treaty of Paris, which ended the war, in 1783.

## Presidency

In 1787 Washington became president of the Constitutional Conveton. Many Americans were suspicious of the idea of a new government, but the fact that Washington was involved encouraged them to support it.

On February 4, 1789, the United States held its first presidential election. Washington received all the votes cast, and John Adams became his vice president.

When Washington took power, the United States faced threats of attack from the British, the Spanish, and Native Americans. The new president made peace with all three and maintained U.S. neutrality when the European nations went to war in 1793.

Later Washington established a financial system to get the United States out of debt. He added new territory in the West and admitted three new states to the Union—Kentucky, Tennessee, and Vermont. He was aided by an able cabinet whose members included Alexander Hamilton and Thomas Jefferson.

After two terms in office Washington retired to Mount Vernon. However, his well-earned retirement was short—he died less than three years later.

SEE ALSO: Adams, John; French & Indian Wars; Hamilton, Alexander; Jefferson, Thomas; Revolution, American; United States of America

## KEY FACTS

**BIRTHPLACE**
Westmoreland County, Virginia

**OCCUPATION**
Planter, soldier

**MARRIED**
Martha Dandridge Custis

**AGE WHEN PRESIDENT**
57

**TERM**
1789–97

**AGE AT DEATH**
67

*Look in the Index for:* *WATCH

## ✳ WATER
Water is the most common substance on Earth, covering almost three-quarters of the planet's surface. All living things depend on it for survival.

Water is composed of two chemical elements, hydrogen (H) and oxygen (O). Each molecule of water consists of two hydrogen atoms and one oxygen atom. Chemists write this formula as $H_2O$.

At normal temperatures water is a liquid. However, it also appears as a solid and as a gas. When its temperature falls below 32°F (0°C), it expands and becomes a solid called ice. When its temperature is raised above 212°F (100°C), water becomes a gas, called vapor or steam. These temperatures are, respectively, the freezing and boiling points of water.

The amount of water on Earth has remained about the same since the planet was formed. But its form is always changing—from solid to li    d, from liquid to gas. and                   ves in a
                             . Heat from
                          ns, lakes,
                          or. Further
                          ts and
                          ools and
                          t form
                          rs to
                          ilstones

                          t salt
                          r is

                          sh

                          ent

to produce crops. For example, 1,000 tons of water are needed to produce just one ton of grain.

### Water and health
During the 20th century the world's human population tripled, and water use increased sixfold. In the same period half the world's wetlands disappeared, and many freshwater fish became endangered. Agriculture uses more water every year to meet the food demands of a growing population. As a result, other users have less and less water. About 5 million people die every year from diseases caused by water pollution or lack of water.

In 1972 the Clean Water Act was passed in the United States. Before then only one-third of U.S. streams, lakes, and coastal waters were clean enough for fishing and swimming. Now two-thirds of our waters are safe.

▲ *Children in Udaipur, India, draw water from a well. In the developing world such sources are not always clean and may cause disease.*

SEE ALSO: Agriculture; Atom & Molecule; Disease; Elements, Chemical; Fish; Glacier; Human Body; Matter; Pollution; Population; Steam; Wetlands

# ✳ WATERFALL
A waterfall is a stream of water that drops sharply from a higher to a lower level. In large falls thousands of gallons pour down every second.

*The world's highest waterfall, Angel Falls on the Churún River in southeast Venezuela.* ▶

Waterfalls usually form when rivers flow over rock that is softer than the surrounding area. Soft rock wears away faster than the hard rock. This creates a ledge, over which the water pours. Waterfalls are also found where glaciers (rivers of ice) have dug valleys deeper than their tributaries or in places where a river channel was raised or lowered.

The amount of water going over a waterfall can vary enormously. If the volume of water is small, it is called a cascade; if large, it is called a cataract. The biggest discharge of water ever recorded was 470,000 cubic ft. (13,300 cu. m) in a second over the Guaíra Falls, between Brazil and Paraguay. However, the falls are now submerged by the Itaipu dam.

### Harnessing the energy
For hundreds of years the fast-flowing water downstream from waterfalls has been used to turn the great stone wheels of mills to grind grain into flour for bread. Today the energy of fast-flowing water is converted into electricity by hydroelectric power plants.

Every year hundreds of thousands of people come to view the most famous falls, such as Niagara Falls on the border of Canada and the United States, Ribbon Fall and Yosemite Falls in California, and Victoria Falls on the border of the African nations of Zambia and Zimbabwe.

## THE WORLD'S HIGHEST WATERFALLS

| | |
|---|---|
| Angel, Venezuela | 3,212 ft. (979m) |
| Tugela, South Africa | 2,800 ft. (853m) |
| Utigord Falls, Norway | 2,625 ft. (800m) |
| Monge Falls, Norway | 2,540 ft. (774m) |
| Mutarazi, Zimbabwe | 2,499 ft. (762m) |
| Yosemite, California | 2,452 ft. (739m) |
| Ostre Mardalofoss, Norway | 2,151 ft. (655m) |
| Tyssestrengene, Norway | 2,123 ft. (647m) |
| Kukenan, Guyana–Venezuela | 2,000 ft. (610m) |
| Sutherland Falls, New Zealand | 1,904 ft. (580m) |

Many waterfalls have several drops; the figures give the total fall.

**SEE ALSO:** Energy; Glacier; River; Water

● *Look in the Index for:* ✳WATER POWER ✳WATT, JAMES

# ⁎ WEIGHTS AND MEASURES

Sometimes it is not enough to say that something is heavy or short or wide. Measurements give the exact dimensions of objects and substances.

*In Indonesia tea pickers are paid according to the weight of leaves that they have harvested.*

As human civilization developed, the need for measurements began. Explorers and soldiers needed to measure distances between places, and traders needed to measure quantities.

### Customary measures

The first measurements were based on the human body. The Romans counted the number of times their right feet went forward. A thousand paces was called *mille passus*, which gives the English word "mile." A cloth merchant measured his goods by stretching them from his nose to his fingertips. People compared small objects with grains of wheat. Larger objects were compared with stones.

The problem with these methods was that the units were not consistent. A tall cloth merchant with long arms would measure more cloth than a short merchant. Grains and stones are not always the same size. A common standard was needed. If two towns were 50 miles apart, everyone had to agree how long a mile was. Gradually people began to develop fixed quantities for measurement. According to legend, the yard is based on the distance from the nose to the fingertip of Henry I, king of England in the 1100s. The measurements of feet, miles, pounds, pints, and so on formed the basis of customary measures. This is the system used today in the United States.

There were still disagreements between different parts of the world. Some of them continue today. For example, a gallon,

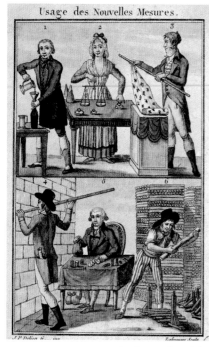

*Usage des Nouvelles Mesures.*

*French workers in the 1790s trying to get used to the new metric system of measurement.*

▶ To convert from customary units of measurement to metric, multiply the number of customary units by the metric figure. For example, 2 in. equals 5cm.

used to measure quantities of liquid, is slightly larger in Britain than in the United States.

As commerce and communications advanced, many people found it hard to see the link between the systems and the objects being measured. It seemed to them unnecessarily complicated that 12 inches should make a foot, 3 feet a yard, 1,760 yards a mile, and so on. They began to look for new, simplified measurements.

### The metric system

In the 1790s French scientists developed a new system. They wanted a set of measurements that would be easier to understand and the same around the world. They decided to make the units fit together in multiples of 10 to make calculations easier. The system they came up with is called the *Système International d'Unités*— International System of Units—or SI. The units they developed were based on specific measurements. A meter was defined as $\frac{1}{40,000,000}$ of the circumference of the Earth. Later calculations showed that their measurement of the Earth was wrong, but the meter remained the same.

Larger and smaller metric units were also based on factors of 10. A centimeter

*A six-foot tape measure. The distance between each of the lines marked is $\frac{1}{32}$nd of an inch.*

▶

## CONVERSIONS

| Customary | Metric |
| --- | --- |
| 1 inch | 2.54cm |
| 1 foot | 30.48cm |
| 1 yard | 91.44cm |
| 1 mile | 1.609km |
| 1 square inch | 6.45 sq. cm |
| 1 square foot | 0.09 sq. m |
| 1 square yard | 0.83 sq. m |
| 1 square mile | 2.59 sq. km |
| 1 acre | 0.4 ha. |
| 1 ounce | 31.1g |
| 1 pound | 0.37kg |
| 1 fluid ounce | 29.57ml |
| 1 pint | 473.2ml |
| 1 gallon | 3.78l |

is one hundredth of a meter. A kilometer is 1,000 meters (about 1,094 yards). The SI unit of weight, or mass, is a gram. It was originally defined as the mass of one cubic centimeter of water. Its name is derived from the Latin word *gramma*, meaning "little weight."

Over the next 200 years the metric system became standard in most of the world. The United States is one of the few countries that still prefers the old systems of weights and measures, although even here the metric system is increasingly used by sports authorities and scientists.

SEE ALSO: Math & Numbers

✳WEST AFRICA 🔎➔ ✳AFRICA, WEST

# * WEST, THE AMERICAN
### In the 19th century American pioneers pushed west of the Mississippi River and braved harsh conditions in search of a better life.

The settlement of the lands west of the Mississippi River began around 1815. The lands in the east were becoming crowded. Explorers and fur trappers, meanwhile, told romantic stories of the West: the Great Plains, the Rocky Mountains, the southwestern deserts, and the Pacific Coast. Many Americans came to believe that it was the destiny, or fate, of the United States to spread all the way across North America. The West seemed to be a place of promise and opportunity, prompting newspaper editor Horace Greeley (1811–72) to coin the phrase "Go west, young man."

### Westward bound

A steady flow of pioneers set off west in wagon trains. Many were farmers, but others hoped to earn a living as storekeepers, reporters, preachers, even actors. Gold and silver were discovered in California and the Rockies in the 1840s and 1850s.

Many miners hurried to the mountains. They lived in violent mining towns without any laws or sheriffs.

The growth of mining and trade spurred the construction of the railroad. In 1869 a line linked the East and West coasts, as well as many of the towns along the way. Telegraph lines also spread across the country, linking East and West.

### Cattle country

The last great region to be settled was the Plains, home to the most famous figures of the West, the cowboys. After the Civil War (1861–65) ranchers in Texas began to drive their longhorn cattle north to graze the grasslands of Kansas, Nebraska, Colorado, Wyoming, Montana, and the Dakotas. The ranchers hired cowboys to drive the herds to "cow towns," such as Dodge City and Abilene, Kansas, where the cattle were loaded onto railroad cars and shipped to stockyards in the eastern cities. Life in the cow towns was rowdy. Town marshals and county sheriffs were appointed to keep the peace, but many of the lawmen were corrupt.

*A cowboy in South Dakota during the late 1880s. Despite the romantic image later created by Hollywood, cowboys spent most of their time doing work that was difficult, dirty, and often boring.*

The Western outlaw gang known as The Wild Bunch. Left to right: Harry Longabaugh ("The Sundance Kid"); William Carver; Ben Kilpatrick ("The Tall Texan"); Harvey Logan ("Kid Curry"); Robert LeRoy Parker ("Butch Cassidy").

During the 1890s and early 1900s there were many criminals in the West—among the most famous were Butch Cassidy, a horse thief, and the James brothers, who robbed trains.

The settlers faced many dangers, including attack by Native Americans who tried to protect their traditional lands from the newcomers. The spread of miners into the Black Hills of the Dakotas in 1874, for example, was resisted by the Sioux. At the Battle of the Little Bighorn in 1876 the Sioux killed about 200 cavalry led by Colonel George A. Custer. But even the Sioux were eventually overwhelmed. The Native Americans were later confined to reservations.

### Homesteaders
A new wave of settlers began to arrive in the West in the 1860s enticed by the 1862 Homestead Act, which allocated western land at little or no cost. (A homestead is an area of land granted to a settler.) Many thousands of people took up the government offer. Among them were numerous white Americans, black former slaves, and poor immigrants from Europe. They went west with high hopes of a better future with political freedom, economic opportunity, or fertile farmland.

But when they got there, the new settlers were often disappointed by the tough prairie soil and the savage climate. The grassland was scorched in summer and blasted by blizzards in winter. Rains were unpredictable. Families lived in sod shacks made from "bricks" of earth, which often had neither plumbing nor nearby roads. Homes were often miles apart, and the work was hard. Droughts in the 1860s and grasshopper plagues in the 1870s wiped out their crops.

Many homesteaders found themselves facing gunmen hired by wealthy cattle ranchers. The cattlemen regarded the newcomers as rustlers (thieves) and outlaws. They did not want homesteaders to fence in the range where their herds grazed. Fighting broke out in so-called "range wars" in Wyoming and Montana. Yet by the end of the 19th century the homesteaders had won. The open range had gone forever.

### End of the wild frontier
Most people today know about the West from movies. Movies show the "Wild West" as a land of cowboys, Indians, and gunfighters. The heroes and heroines are strong and independent. They can look out for themselves. They are quiet and private. They are honest even where there are no laws and no sheriffs. They are smart and good at fixing things. Those are qualities that many Americans still think are important. They believe that the pioneers and cowboys helped build America. The truth was less romantic than the movies. Life for many people in the West was hard, lonely, and often very poor. The pioneers, however, certainly did have to be hardy and self-reliant.

SEE ALSO: Chief Joseph; Colonial America; Cowboy; Crazy Horse; Frontier, The American; Native Americans, Plains; Native Americans, Southwest; United States of America

# ✳ WEST VIRGINIA

Originally part of Virginia, the east–central state of West Virginia became a separate state in 1863 during the Civil War (1861–65).

West Virginia has an irregular shape. Two branches of land stick out to the north and east. They are generally known as the Northern Panhandle—between Ohio and Pennsylvania—and the Eastern Panhandle—between Maryland and Virginia. Rugged mountains and winding rivers form most of West Virginia's borders. The Ohio River makes a boundary between West Virginia and Ohio. The Potomac River separates West Virginia from Maryland.

The Allegheny Plateau covers about 80 percent of the state. It rises from the Ohio River Valley in the west to the rugged Allegheny Mountains, part of the Appalachian Highlands, in the east. Streams have cut deep gorges in much of the Allegheny Plateau, creating a rough and broken countryside.

Most of the Eastern Panhandle is made up of a series of parallel ridges and valleys. The Blue Ridge mountain range runs through the easternmost part of the panhandle.

West Virginia has humid, hot summers and cold winters. In July the temperature averages 73°F (23°C), but it can get much hotter. In January the statewide average is 33°F (1°C), but temperatures are lower in

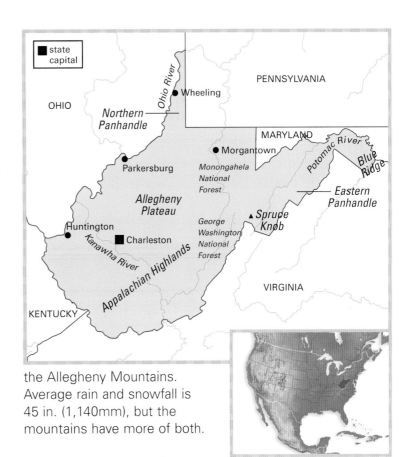

the Allegheny Mountains. Average rain and snowfall is 45 in. (1,140mm), but the mountains have more of both.

## Plant and animal life

More than 75 percent of the total area of West Virginia is covered with trees. State and national forests contain oak, maple, beech, yellow birch, hemlock, spruce, and pine. Flowering shrubs such as mountain laurel and rhododendrons grow in the mountains, as do sundews, bog rosemary, and other unusual wild plants.

Conservation programs have helped West Virginia maintain a wide variety of forest animals, game birds, and fish. Black bears live in the Monongahela National Forest, and whitetail deer are plentiful. Small animals include raccoons, minks, skunks, woodchucks, opossums, and foxes. More than 300 species of birds nest in West Virginia. Game birds include wild turkeys and ruffed grouse.

**West Virginia's state flag**

*A mine in West Virginia. Coal is one of the most important products of the state's economy.*
◄

## KEY FACTS

**AREA**
24,231 sq. mi.
(62,759 sq. km);
rank, 41st

**POPULATION**
1,808,344 (2000
census); rank, 37th

**ELEVATION**
Highest—4,861 ft.
(1,483m) at Spruce
Knob; lowest—240
ft. (72m) along the
Potomac River

**CAPITAL**
Charleston

**STATEHOOD**
June 20, 1863;
35th state

**ABBREVIATION**
WV

**STATE MOTTO**
Mountaineers are
always free

**STATE SONG**
"West Virginia
Hills"

**STATE
NICKNAME**
Mountain State

**STATE FLOWER**
Great
rhododendron

**STATE TREE**
Sugar maple

**STATE BIRD**
Cardinal

### People

Many West Virginians trace their roots to the early settlers, who were mainly English, German, Scottish, or Irish. Others are descendants of Italians, Hungarians, Poles, Irish, and Russians who came to mine coal and work in other industries. Thousands of African Americans came from the southern states.

The most densely populated areas of the state are in the industrialized Ohio, Kanawha, and Monongahela valleys and in the Eastern Panhandle.

### Economy

West Virginia's early settlers were farmers. Gradually people also turned to mining and manufacturing. Farming is still important today, although many farmers also have other jobs. Since the mid-1930s West Virginia has been a major producer of coal. The state is also an important source of natural gas and petroleum.

### History

Although many ancient burial grounds and artifacts have been found in West Virginia, by the time Europeans arrived in the late 1600s, very few Native Americans were still living there. No one knows for sure why they abandoned the land—it may have been because of disease or war.

The Iroquois, Cherokee, and Shawnee continued to claim the area as desirable hunting ground.

From 1624 to 1776 all of Virginia was an English colony. There is no record of when the first settlement was made in West Virginia, but it was probably about 1730.

Differences existed between east and west Virginia from the earliest times— over slavery, education, the building of roads and canals, taxes, and other issues. In 1861 the Civil War brought new conflicts. Most eastern Virginians were in favor of slavery, and they seceded from (left) the Union. The western counties remained in the Union, and in 1863 they became the state of West Virginia.

One of the most remarkable things about West Virginia's first 50 years of statehood was its rapid industrial development. Industries based on natural resources—coal, oil, gas, and timber—grew the fastest. Many people came from Europe to find work.

Recently new highways and other improvements have attracted new industries, such as tourism. People who moved away from the state during periods of high unemployment in the 1900s have begun to move back. Today West Virginians are proud of their low crime rate and relaxed way of life.

*The New River gorge in rural West Virginia.* ▶

**SEE ALSO:** Civil War; Virginia

# ✱ WETLANDS

**A wetland is an area where the soil is saturated (wet through) with water or covered by shallow pools of water for long periods of time.**

Wetlands cover 6 percent of the Earth's land surface and are found in all countries and in all climates. They include swamps, bogs, and marshes.

## Swamps

Swamps are forested wetlands. In shallow-water swamps the ground stays moist all year. Deep-water swamps form along rivers and often flood. Along the seacoasts of tropical areas saltwater swamps sometimes form. Some trees in swamps grow right out of the water. Others grow on small islands called hummocks. The animal and plant species that thrive in swamps vary. Hemlock and willow trees are both suited to wet ground. Mangrove trees can survive in both salty and freshwater environments.

## Bogs

Bogs are usually found in northern regions in the depressions left by glaciers (rivers of ice). Water settles in the depressions, and plants take root. Because of poor drainage plant matter does not decay fully. Spongy moss grows on the surface of the water. A brown material called peat builds up below the surface. Wood frogs and some small mammals thrive in bogs.

## Marshes

The main vegetation in marshes is soft-stemmed plants called emergents. Saw grass, wild rice, and rushes are examples. Emergents grow with part of their stems below the water and the tops above the

*Cypress Creek National Wildlife Refuge provides a habitat for many animals that are in danger of becoming extinct (dying out).*

surface. Marshes are an important habitat for many kinds of fish, birds, such as herons, and otters and beavers.

**The importance of wetlands**

Most wetlands provide habitats for a wide variety of wildlife. Many species are only found in swamps, bogs, or marshes. Humans also benefit from these environments, raising fish and growing crops. Rice grows in marshes. Wetlands control flooding and also prevent erosion. Laws have maintained some wetlands as conservation areas, but people have already destroyed about half the world's natural wetlands. They have been drained and built over for roads, houses, and factories, for example.

**SEE ALSO:** Biome; Environment; Extinction; Glacier; Habitat; Water

## ✱WHALE AND DOLPHIN 👀 ✱SEA MAMMAL

# ✳ WILDER, LAURA INGALLS (1867–1957)

Laura Ingalls Wilder was the author of the "Little House" series of books on American pioneer life. She received many awards and honors for her books.

*Laura Wilder wrote about her family's adventures on the American frontier.*

The Ingalls family lived in a log cabin in Wisconsin. Laura was the second of four sisters. From 1869 to 1879 the family traveled by covered wagon throughout the Midwest in search of productive land. Wilder's first memories were of their move to Kansas. They finally settled on a homestead in South Dakota in 1880.

When she was in her forties, Wilder started writing for regional magazines and newspapers. At the age of 65 she published her first novel, *Little House in the Big Woods*. Popular demand led her to write eight more books based on the story of the family's adventures.

Wilder's books made her internationally famous. They were widely used in schools to teach about frontier life. During her lifetime she answered thousands of letters from admiring readers. She died at her Missouri farm at age 90.

A popular television series in the 1970s and 1980s, *Little House on the Prairie*, was loosely based on Wilder's stories. All her former homes have been restored to honor her life and work.

**SEE ALSO:** Biography & Autobiography; Frontier, The American

# ✳ WILSON, THOMAS WOODROW (1856–1924)

Thomas Woodrow Wilson was the 28th president of the United States from 1913 to 1921. He took the nation into World War I (1914–18).

*Woodrow Wilson was one of the great presidents of the United States. At home he oversaw the passage of a number of important laws, while in Europe he was hailed as a hero at the end of World War I.*

Wilson was born on December 28 or 29, 1856 (he always gave December 28 as his birthday, but the Wilson family Bible indicated that he was born about 12:45 A.M on December 29), the son of a Presbyterian minister. He graduated from the College of New Jersey, which later became Princeton University, in 1879 and studied law at the University of Virginia. Ill health forced him to withdraw in 1880, but he completed his studies at home.

After a failed attempt to practice as a lawyer, he became a university teacher. In 1902 he became president of Princeton University before starting on a new career in politics. He left Princeton in 1910 to fight his first political campaign for the governorship of New Jersey.

In 1912 he ran for the Democratic presidential nomination. He won on the 46th ballot. A major part of his campaign program was tariff (import tax) reform. The Republican vote was split between President Taft and former president Theodore Roosevelt's Progressive, or Bull Moose, Party. Wilson won 435 of the 529 electoral votes.

## Presidency

Wilson was the first Democratic president in 16 years. That meant that he had few experienced people for his new cabinet and had to fill many roles himself.

He reduced tariff rates, brought in an income tax, and introduced new controls on businesses. He also passed the Child Labor Act, which stopped children under 14 from working in factories. But Wilson's main impact was in foreign affairs. He sent troops to Mexico, Nicaragua, Haiti, and the Dominican Republic to restore stability and to protect U.S. interests.

In 1914 many European nations began the conflict that would become known as World War I. Wilson, in common with most Americans, wanted to stay neutral. He fought for, and won, a second term of office on a platform of "peace and progressivism." But Germany's behavior, including attacks on passenger ships,

alarmed him. In April 1917 he won the support of Congress for a declaration of war. He raised an army of two million men that helped turn the tide of the war in favor of Britain and its allies.

Wilson led the U.S. delegation to the Paris peace conference, and he pushed for the creation of the League of Nations, an international body that would prevent future wars. When he got back home, Wilson delivered 40 speeches in support of the League. In October 1919 he suffered a stroke. In his absence the Senate voted against the United States joining the League. Wilson was awarded the Nobel Peace Prize the same year.

SEE ALSO: Nobel Prize; Roosevelt, Theodore; Taft, William H.; World War I

# ✳ WIND

**Wind is the effect of air moving because of changes in air temperature or pressure. Wind can provide benefits, but it can also be very destructive.**

Several factors cause air to move. One is temperature. Warm air is lighter than cold air, so it rises. A nearby area of cold air will move to replace the risen air. A region of air movement is called a circulation cell.

Air pressure also produces wind. When two places close together have different levels of air pressure, air moves from the high-pressure area to the low-pressure area. The greater the difference in pressure, the stronger the wind.

### Types of wind

Scientists classify winds in various ways. The Beaufort scale measures wind speed based on how it affects the surface of the sea. On land an instrument called an anemometer converts wind into electrical current. A stronger current indicates a greater wind speed. Winds between 32

A tornado strikes Phuket Island, Thailand.

and 63 mph (51–101 km/h) are called gale force winds. At speeds of over 74 mph (119 km/h) a wind is at hurricane force.

Winds also blow in patterns called wind systems. The gentlest of them are called breezes. They are caused by circulation

## AMAZING FACTS!

**One of the world's fastest winds** was recorded at Mount Washington, New Hampshire, on April 12, 1934. It reached a speed of 231 mph (372km/h).

cells. In coastal areas breezes often come in from the ocean because the air is cooler above the sea than above the land.

Some winds are stronger. Thunder storms form when downdrafts strike the ground. Wind speeds of 50 mph (80km/h) or more can occur. Tornadoes, monsoons, and other large storms are accompanied by even stronger winds.

Strong winds and storms can cause massive destruction. Winds combined with cold weather can create an effect called wind chill, which can kill people.

However, winds can also make the Earth more habitable for people and other species. They reduce the heat of the tropical regions and warm the polar areas with air from the tropics. They also aid in the evaporation and movement of water.

In recent years people have harnessed winds to provide new sources of energy. Large groups of windmills produce electricity in California and other areas. This is a renewable energy source, since the Earth can never exhaust the supply.

**SEE ALSO:** Climate & Weather; Electricity; Energy; Hurricane, Tornado, & Typhoon; Natural Resources; Water

---

## *WIND INSTRUMENTS 👀 *MUSICAL INSTRUMENTS

---

# *WISCONSIN

**Wisconsin is a midwestern state. It borders the Mississippi River in the west and two of the Great Lakes, Superior and Michigan, to the north and east.**

Every year thousands of tourists flock to Wisconsin to enjoy its lakes, forests, and other scenic attractions. The landscape is varied, with grassy plains, mountains, and a variety of features created by glaciers (rivers of ice). During the ice age huge glaciers scraped off hilltops and filled in valleys with loose earth materials. The glaciers created the Great Lakes.

The state is veined with thousands of miles of rivers and streams. The largest lake is

*The American badger lives in Wisconsin's forests and is often regarded as the state animal.*

Winnebago in the Fox River Valley. Lake Geneva in southern Wisconsin is a popular vacation resort.

Summers in southern Wisconsin can be hot and muggy, while winters along the northern border can be cold with heavy snowfall. Average temperatures in July range from 65°F (18°C) in the north to 75°F (24°C) in the south and in January from 7°F (14°C) to 24°F (4°C). Average rain and snowfall is about 30 in. (760mm) a year.

● **Look in the Index for:** *WIND POWER

## Plant and animal life

Nearly half of Wisconsin is forested. Trees include oak, hickory, aspen, birch, and spruce. Foxes, beavers, muskrats, and badgers are found throughout the state. It is estimated that Wisconsin is home to more than a million deer. Black bears and raccoons thrive in the woodlands, and coyotes howl at night. Elk have been reintroduced to the woods, and the bald eagle population is being restored.

## People

When French explorers and fur traders first arrived in Wisconsin in the 1600s, Winnebago, Menominee, and other Native Americans lived there. The first large wave of white settlement began in about 1820, when people from Tennessee and Kentucky flocked to southwestern Wisconsin to farm. Immigration from Europe began about 1835 and included large groups of Germans and Poles. Today Native Americans make up less than 1 percent of the population.

## Economy

Southern Wisconsin produces a third of the nation's cheese and more butter than any other state. Its license plates proclaim it America's Dairyland, an apt name for the state with the most dairy cows in the nation. Over half of Wisconsin's income comes from service industries, such as banking, insurance, and tourism. Manufacturing plays an important role in the economy. Wisconsin leads all other states in the manufacture of small gasoline engines, power cranes, mining machinery, and other types of industrial equipment.

## History

About 12,000 years ago small bands of hunters followed herds of giant bison, elk, and wooly mammoths into the area that is now Wisconsin. By A.D. 500 Native Americans lived in the area.

*Farm buildings at Chippahua Falls, Wisconsin. Although the state has a large number of farms, agriculture supplies only a small percentage of Wisconsin's income.*

## KEY FACTS

**AREA**
65,499 sq. mi. (169,643 sq. km); rank, 22nd

**POPULATION**
5,363,675 (2000 census); rank, 18th

**ELEVATION**
Highest—1,952 ft. (595m) at Timms Hill; lowest—581 ft. (177m) along Lake Michigan

**CAPITAL**
Madison

**STATEHOOD**
May 29, 1848; 30th state

**ABBREVIATION**
WI

**STATE MOTTO**
Forward

**STATE SONG**
"On, Wisconsin!"

**STATE NICKNAME**
Badger State

**STATE FLOWER**
Wood violet

**STATE TREE**
Sugar maple

**STATE BIRD**
Robin

**Wisconsin's state flag**

French explorer Jean Nicolet was the first European to set foot in Wisconsin in 1634. In 1672 Wisconsin was declared part of the Kingdom of France. French explorers, fur traders, and missionaries moved into the area. Between 1712 and 1738 there were a series of battles between the French and the Native Americans. One hundred years of French rule came to an end in 1763 after the French and Indian Wars, and Britain gained control of the area.

Twenty years later the United States took control after defeating Britain in the American Revolution (1775–83). In 1836 settlers formed the Wisconsin Territory. In 1848 Wisconsin joined the Union.

During the Civil War (1861–65) the state lost 12,000 men fighting for the Union. After the war the state's industry and agriculture expanded. During this period most laborers worked long hours for little pay. Laws to protect the rights of workers were introduced in 1911. Wisconsin was the first state to provide financial assistance to the disabled, to children, and to the unemployed.

**SEE ALSO:** Civil War; Exploration & Explorers; French & Indian Wars; Glacier; Revolution, American; Slavery

*WOLF see *DOG

# *WOMEN'S RIGHTS MOVEMENT

**For most of history, and in most cultures, women have not enjoyed the same rights as men. The first campaigns for women's rights began in the 1800s.**

*Mary Wollstonecraft Godwin, a founder of the modern feminist movement. She argued that women should enjoy the same rights as men.*

Until the late 1800s western women were second-class citizens. They could not vote. It was very difficult for them to enter college or a profession. If they married, all their property belonged to their husbands.

One of the most important thinkers in the early women's movement was Mary Wollstonecraft Godwin (1759–97). In her book *Vindication of the Rights of Woman* she argued that women should have equal rights in marriage, politics, and education.

The first meeting for women's rights in the United States took place in 1848, at Seneca Falls, New York. The organizers presented a "Declaration of Rights and Sentiments." It was based on the Declaration of Independence but announced that "all men and women are created equal."

The early leaders of the American women's movement were Susan B. Anthony, Elizabeth Cady Stanton, and Lucy Stone. They pressured state legislatures to reform voting and property laws. Many campaigners for women's rights were also involved in the struggle to abolish slavery.

Gradually women began to win property rights and the right to attend college. They could also vote in some states. By the

*Campaigners for women's right to vote, known as suffragists, march in front of the Capitol in Washington, D.C., in 1913.*

early 1900s many other countries had overtaken the United States in the freedoms that women had won. The National Woman's Party, founded in 1913, took radical action in its campaigning for women's rights. The NWP called for a picket of the White House, and 168 women were imprisoned. But it was not until 1920 that the 19th Amendment was passed permitting women to vote in all elections.

### The battle for equality

Alice Paul, one of the founders of the NWP, carried on the campaign for women's rights after the 19th Amendment was passed. In 1923 she drafted the first version of the Equal Rights Amendment. It stated simply: "Men and women shall have equal rights throughout the United States and every place subject to its jurisdiction." It was introduced to Congress but did not pass.

By the end of World War II, in 1945, women had the vote in most democratic countries. However, they were nowhere near equality with men. Employers were allowed to pay women less than men for the same work. Some professions and organizations were still closed to women. Women were often expected to stop working when they became mothers.

The campaign for full equality between men and women became a major force throughout the world during the 1960s. The first female political leaders of countries took power in Sri Lanka and India. Writers such as Simone de Beauvoir, Germaine Greer, and Betty Friedan publicized the ideas of women's rights and led the campaign. People began to use a new word for these arguments—feminism.

## DID YOU KNOW?

The United Nations Convention on the Elimination of All Forms of Discrimination Against Women became an international treaty in 1981. It calls for the abolition of women's slavery, equal access to education and employment opportunities, maternity leave, and the right to control the number and spacing of children.

President John F. Kennedy ordered federal agencies to treat men and women equally in employment. In 1963 he signed the Equal Pay Act, which meant that employers had to pay men and women the same amount for the same work.

The 1964 Civil Rights Act was intended to give rights to African Americans and other ethnic groups. But Alice Paul and other campaigners succeeded in also protecting equality for women. The Equal Employment Opportunity Commission was set up to enforce these laws.

In 1966 a new group, the National Organization for Women (NOW), was founded. It began a campaign to put Alice Paul's Equal Rights Amendment into law. The campaign failed but increased publicity for the argument that women and men should be treated equally.

**Women's rights around the world**
In North America, Europe, and other parts of the world women's rights are now guaranteed by law. But in many countries religious or economic restrictions mean that women are still second-class citizens. Campaigners disagree about whether the west should force these countries to accept women's rights—or whether this is forcing western ideals onto other cultures.

SEE ALSO: Abolitionist Movement; Anthony, Susan B.; Constitution; Declaration of Independence; Stanton, Elizabeth Cady; United Nations; Women's Suffrage

# ✳ WOMEN'S SUFFRAGE

Suffrage is the right to vote. For many years men in democratic countries had the right to vote for leaders and governments, while women did not.

*In 1912 Ohio suffragists tried to persuade people to vote for an amendment to Ohio's constitution proposing women's suffrage. However, their campaign failed.*

In some democracies at the start of the 1800s many men did not have the vote. In the United States slaves could not vote. In the United Kingdom and other countries people could be stopped from voting if they did not own land, or if they followed a particular religion. However, by the second half of the century all men were able to vote in most democratic countries. But women still did not have the vote. Some people thought that women were not intelligent enough to vote. Others thought that if women became involved in politics, they would not want to be wives or mothers.

Women's suffrage was one of the main demands of campaigners for women's rights in the 1800s and early 1900s. Women such as Emmeline Pankhurst in the United Kingdom were prepared to go to prison to support their struggle. New Zealand gave women the vote in 1893.

World War I (1914–18) was a major turning point. Many women worked in factories and took over "male" jobs. They argued that if they could be equal with men in industry, they should have equal rights to vote. By 1919, 15 countries had given women the vote, including the United Kingdom, Canada, Germany, and Russia.

**Campaigns in the United States**
Women met at Seneca Falls, New York, in 1848 and made suffrage a core part of their campaign. Supporters of women's suffrage and the abolition of slavery often supported each other's claims. However, after the end of the Civil War in 1865 some abolitionists withdrew their support.

The National American Woman Suffrage Association formed in 1890. By 1900 four states—Colorado, Idaho, Utah, and Wyoming—had given the vote to women. But an amendment to the Constitution was needed to ensure that women in all states could vote. In 1917 President Woodrow Wilson gave his backing to an amendment ensuring votes for women. The 19th Amendment, giving the vote to women, was finally ratified in 1920.

SEE ALSO: Constitution; Election; Government; Women's Rights Movement

# *WOODWIND 👓 *MUSICAL INSTRUMENTS
# *WOOL 👓 *TEXTILE

# * WORLD TRADE CENTER

For many years the twin towers of the World Trade Center dominated the skyline of New York City. They were destroyed in the terrorist attacks of 2001.

The World Trade Center was built between 1966 and 1972. The architect was Minoru Yamasaki in cooperation with Emery Roth & Sons. Because of the great height of the towers the designers had to make them rigid to cope with the force of strong winds. Each floor was trussed to the walls at the corners, to prevent the buildings from bending and swaying.

When the 110 story-towers opened in 1973, they were 1,368 ft. (417m) and 1,362 (415m) tall and held 13 million sq. ft. (1.2 million sq. m) of office space. They cost an estimated $1.5 billion and were the tallest skyscrapers in the world. However, the Sears Tower in Chicago, Illinois, broke the record the following year at

*The Twin Towers dominated the New York skyline before their destruction in September 2001.*

● *Look in the Index for:* *WORK

1,454 ft. (443m) tall. The Twin Towers remained the tallest structures in New York City.

### Attacks on the towers

On February 26, 1993, a bomb exploded in an underground garage in the center. Six people died, and more than 1,000 were injured. Over the next four years six people were convicted of the attacks. They were linked to terrorist groups in the Middle East.

On September 11, 2001, terrorists hijacked four airliners. They flew two of them into the towers of the World Trade Center. Within hours both towers collapsed, and nearly 3,000 people lost their lives. Another airliner caused serious damage to the Pentagon in Arlington, Virginia. The last one was heading for the Capitol, in Washington, D.C., but was brought down by passenger action in a field in Pennsylvania. The chief suspect as mastermind of the attacks was Osama bin Laden, head of the Al Qaeda network, a group of Islamic extremists.

It was the most destructive terrorist act in history and an attack on the American way of life. The American people, and our friends around the world, were thrown into mourning. On September 20, 2001, President George W. Bush announced a War on Terrorism to bring the organizers of the attacks to justice.

SEE ALSO: Architecture; Bush, George W.; Construction; New York; Skyscraper

# ✳ WORLD WAR I

World War I (1914–18) involved more than 30 nations. It claimed more than 14 million lives, devastated Europe, and toppled kings and emperors.

*An American soldier and his horse wear gas masks to protect them against poison gas.*

When war broke out in 1914, there had long been tension between France and Germany, which had fought a war in 1871. By the 1900s Europe formed two hostile camps—France, Russia, and Great Britain on one side, and Germany, Italy, and Austria-Hungary on the other. Germany's kaiser (emperor), Wilhelm II, wanted a great empire to rival that of Great Britain and was preparing to take it by force.

The spark for war came in the Balkans. On June 28, 1914 a Serbian student assassinated Archduke Franz Ferdinand, heir to the throne of Austria-Hungary. Austria attacked Serbia on July 28. Russia was allied to Serbia, and its ally France also prepared for war. Germany sided with Austria and declared war in early August. When German troops marched into neutral Belgium to attack France, Britain entered the war. Japan later joined the Allies (France, Britain, and Russia).

## Western front, 1914

In the west the German plan was to sweep through tiny Belgium into France. The Belgians fought bravely, but the Germans pressed on and advanced almost to Paris, the French capital, by early September. They were stopped at the battle of the Marne. By Christmas the fighting was at stalemate. The front (the zone of fighting) was a shell-cratered maze of trenches and barbed wire stretching 475 miles (765km). Already more than 1.5 million soldiers had died.

## The wider conflict

In the east the Germans had driven back Russian attacks in August and September 1914. In October the Ottoman (Turkish) Empire joined the Central Powers (headed by Germany and Austria-Hungary). The Turks prevented shipping from taking supplies to Russia via the Black Sea, and they defeated all Allied attempts to reopen the route. In 1915 Bulgaria joined the Central Powers and Italy joined the Allies, while in 1916 Romania and Greece also joined the Allied side. Fighting would later spread into the Middle East and Africa.

## Western front, 1915–17

The fighting in the west during 1915 was marked by futile offensives by both sides. Men fell in their thousands, cut down by machine guns or choked by a deadly new German weapon—poison gas. But the front lines did not move as much as 3 miles (5km) in any direction. The British tried to draw pressure off the French by advancing along the Somme River in 1916. They brought a new weapon of their own: the tank. It was in vain, however: At the Battle of the Somme an estimated 1.2 million men died for 5 miles (8km) of land.

The year 1917 was another dark one for the Allies. Attempts to break through the German positions in northern France failed. At the Second Battle of the Aisne parts of the French Army mutinied (refused to obey orders). At the Battle of Passchendaele months of fighting cost the British some 300,000 dead.

## The United States

In 1916 Russia launched a grand offensive against Austria, but after early successes the onslaught ground to a halt, with more than a million Russian soldiers killed. In March 1917 the Russian people overthrew their czar (emperor), Nicholas II, and in November the Communists swept to power. Their leader, Vladimir Lenin, took Russia out of the war in December, 1917.

So far the United States had kept out of the fighting. In 1917, however, German submarines began attacking American shipping. President Woodrow Wilson declared war on Germany, and in June the first American troops landed in France.

## Final stages

By 1918, with Russia out of the war, Germany transferred more than a million troops from the eastern front to the west. On March 21 the Germans launched the enormous "Michael" offensive. Once again they were halted, after terrible loss of life on both sides. By May, however, American troops were at last tipping the balance in the Allies' favor, and bit by bit the German army weakened until it was decisively defeated in the fall.

On September 30 Bulgaria surrendered. Turkey followed on October 30, and Austria on November 3. Finally, on November 11, Germany signed a truce. The war was over.

*British soldiers advance toward German trenches in 1918. The killing power of machine-guns changed the nature of warfare. The guns pinned their targets down in whatever cover could be found or made. This meant that the front lines of the two sides were often separated by only a short distance.*

*German soldiers attack from a trench. Trenches were filthy ditches where soldiers ate, slept, and waited to be sent "over the top" in wave after wave of infantry attack, only to be shot down in a hail of enemy fire.*

## Aftermath

World War I changed the map of Europe and sowed the seeds for World War II. The Ottoman Empire broke up. The Austro-Hungarian Empire crumbled, giving rise to new states, including Czechoslovakia, Yugoslavia, and Poland. Finland, Estonia, Latvia, and Lithuania broke free from the Russian Empire. Through the Treaty of Versailles, signed in France in 1919, the Allied powers blamed Germany for the war, stripped it of land, and ordered it to pay billions of dollars.

**SEE ALSO:** Army; Balkans; Europe; Europe, Central & Eastern; Revolution; Warfare; Wilson, Woodrow; World War II

# ✳ WORLD WAR II

World War II (1939–45) was the most destructive war in history. It involved all the world's great powers and many of the smaller nations.

After the bloodshed of World War I (1914–18) the world's most powerful countries signed treaties that they hoped would create a lasting peace. But economic problems and political tensions between the traditional ruling groups, the middle classes, and revolutionary communist parties ravaged much of central Europe. In 1933 an ambitious ex-soldier, Adolf Hitler, came to power in Germany. He blamed Germany's defeat in World War I on a Jewish plot. He ruled as a dictator (leader with total power) at the head of his National Socialist (or Nazi) Party and steadily built up Germany's armed forces.

Other brutal dictators also rose to power after World War I: Benito Mussolini in Italy and military leaders in Japan, including Tojo Hideki. Italy and Japan would fight alongside Germany as the major Axis powers.

## War breaks out

Hitler, Mussolini, and Japan's leaders all wanted to build great empires. During the 1930s Japan invaded eastern China, and Italy invaded Ethiopia in East Africa. Germany swallowed up the Rhineland, its neighbor Austria, and Czechoslovakia. When Hitler invaded Poland in September 1939, Britain and France declared war on Germany. But Germany swiftly conquered Poland, helped by the Soviet Union.

Hitler's armies were the finest in Europe. Their fighting tactics were called Blitzkrieg ("lightning war"). In spring 1940 they overran Belgium, the Netherlands, Luxembourg, Norway, and Denmark. Winston Churchill became prime minister of Great Britain on May 10. Three days later the Germans invaded France. Only the British Royal Air Force and Royal Navy stopped Germany from crossing the English Channel and attacking England.

Mussolini, meanwhile, had invaded Albania in 1939. In 1940 he attacked British-held Egypt from his colony in Libya, but the Italians were fiercely opposed by British forces, and Hitler was forced to send German military support.

### The eastern front

In spring 1941 Hitler attacked the Balkans, and then on June 22, 1941, he marched into the Soviet Union. German troops and armor rolled victoriously across the vast land until the fall, when rain made their progress slower. They reached the suburbs of Moscow in December 1941. Russian counterattack and the winter cold halted them. By the fall of 1942 German forces had reached the city of Stalingrad.

### America and the Pacific

The United States had lent warships to Britain to help defeat the U-boats (German submarines) that were sinking Allied supply ships in the North Atlantic Ocean. Otherwise it had deliberately kept out of the conflict. Then, on December 7, 1941, Japanese aircraft attacked the U.S. Pacific fleet at its base in Pearl Harbor, Hawaii. Two days later the United States entered the war.

Japan mounted offensives in the Pacific and controlled much of southeastern Asia by May 1942. From that point, however,

U.S. naval forces began to hit back. The battles of the Coral Sea in May and Midway in early June severely damaged Japan's vital aircraft carrier fleet.

### Europe and North Africa

By 1943 the tide had begun to turn against Hitler in Europe. Allied aircraft were pounding Axis factories and supply routes. Soviet troops had surrounded and destroyed the German Sixth Army at Stalingrad. Axis troops in North Africa were finally defeated in May 1943.

### The Allies invade Europe

From July 1943 Allied troops invaded and fought their way up through Italy, finally taking Rome in June 1944. On June 6, "D-Day," American, British, and Canadian forces landed in Normandy, France. Weeks of bitter fighting followed. They freed Paris on August 25 and pressed on to reach the German border by October. The Soviet Red Army, which had been steadily advancing west, reached the

*British fighter planes, known as Spitfires, flying in formation at over 300 miles (480km) per hour.*

*Supplies arrive for U.S. Marines on the Japanese-held island of Iwo Jima. The island was of vital importance in the battle between the United States and Japan in 1945.*

outskirts of Berlin in April 1945. Hitler committed suicide on the 30th. Two days earlier Italian freedom fighters had shot Mussolini, and Italy's war was over. Germany surrendered on May 7.

After the fighting ended in Europe, war still raged in the Pacific between the Allies and the Japanese. To end the bloodshed as swiftly as possible, President Harry S. Truman gave the order to drop atomic bombs on the Japanese cities of Hiroshima and Nagasaki on August 6 and 9, 1945. The two explosions instantly killed over 150,000 people. Japan surrendered on September 2.

### Aftermath

World War II has been called a "total war." Land, sea, and air forces all played their part. Civilians were deliberately killed.

Perhaps the worst aspect of the war on civilians was the attempt by followers of Hitler to wipe out Europe's Jews during the Holocaust. The use of atomic weapons took the political world into a dangerous new age. The United States, its economy boosted by the war, was now a superpower. Europe, which had once ruled the world, lay in ruins. In the years to come European colonies in Africa and Asia would rush to claim independence.

**SEE ALSO:** Dictatorship.; Germany; Hitler, Adolf; Holocaust; Italy; Japan; Roosevelt, Franklin D; Russia & the Baltic States; Truman, Harry S.; United Kingdom; United States of America; Warfare; World War I

# ✳ WORM

Worms are invertebrates—animals without backbones—with soft, long bodies. They can live on land, in water, and even in other animals.

The most familiar type of worm is the earthworm. It is an annelid, a word meaning "small rings." The body of an annelid is divided into small segments, or rings. An earthworm has no eyes or ears and spends most of its time underground. It burrows through the ground, taking soil into an inner digestive tube that runs the length of its body. It takes nutrition from plant and animal matter in the soil, and discards the rest. This process turns and aerates the soil, which is why earthworms are so important to farmers.

The largest group of annelids are bristle worms. Most bristle worms have tiny eyes and hard jaws. They often live in tubes made in sand or soil, or from a hard, limey substance made by the worm itself.

*The brandling worm is an annelid with small rings, or segments. They are used by gardeners to make compost heaps and by fishermen as bait.*

Ragworms and bloodworms are part of this group. Leeches are also annelids. They have smooth bodies with suckers at each end. They attach themselves to live animals, including humans, and suck out blood for food. This is called parasitism.

### Roundworms

Roundworms, or nematodes, have digestive tubes inside an outer body tube, like annelids. However, the body is not segmented. Most roundworms are tiny, although some can grow to 3 ft. (1m) long. Many live in soil or water, but some, such as the hookworm, can enter the human body. Hookworms are parasites, entering the intestines and sucking blood.

### Flatworms

Planarians, flukes, and tapeworms are all flatworms. Most flatworms are small and thin. Planarians usually live in shallow water, feeding on tiny animals. They can be found under stones in clear water or gliding over the sand in shallow salt water. Flukes and tapeworms are parasites. They feed on the body fluids and tissues of their hosts such as a sheep or a pig. Flukes and tapeworms can enter the human body and live on body fluids, causing damage to the internal organs.

SEE ALSO: Animal; Invertebrate

# ✳ WRIGHT, FRANK LLOYD (1867–1959)

Some people believe Frank Lloyd Wright was the most important American architect in history. His buildings still influence modern designers.

Wright was born in Richland Center, Wisconsin, on June 8, 1867. His mother gave him wooden blocks and shaped cards to play with, and that gave him an early interest in building things.

Wright moved to Chicago, where he worked for the architect Louis Sullivan, whom he called "Master." In 1893 Wright opened his own office.

When designing buildings, Wright followed the rule that "form follows function." This means that the needs of a building's users should determine its structure, not rules laid down by architects in the past. Many of Wright's creations were shocking to people used to more conservative designs.

They were often low and flat, and seemed to blend in with their natural surroundings. Wright was also one of the first architects to use concrete as the main material for construction without disguising it under other materials.

By the end of Wright's long life he had designed buildings in 36 states. His fame spread in Europe earlier than the United States. Colleagues did not always get on with him, finding him stubborn and arrogant. But even his enemies acknowledged his importance and influence as an architect.

*Frank Lloyd Wright designed more than 400 buildings during a career that lasted 70 years. He designed his own home and studio in Arizona.*

SEE ALSO: Architecture; Construction; Design

# ☀ WRIGHT, ORVILLE AND WILBUR

**The Wright brothers invented the first power-driven airplane. Other people had flown in balloons and gliders, but they were the first to build an airplane.**

The Wright Brothers invented the first airplane. Wilbur Wright (left) flew about 120 feet (36.5m) on the beach at Kitty Hawk on the North Carolina coast.

Wilbur Wright was born in Milville, Indiana, on April 16, 1867. Orville was born in Dayton, Ohio, on August 19, 1871. From childhood the brothers were greatly interested in mechanics.

In 1889 Orville started a printing business using a press he had made. Wilbur joined the business, and it did very well. In 1893, when bicycling became popular, the brothers decided to open a bicycle repair shop. Eventually they built and sold bicycles as well as repairing them.

The brothers had long been fascinated by the idea of flight. After experimenting with box kites, they built a glider that looked like a big box kite with two wings. They took their glider to Kitty Hawk on the North Carolina coast in the fall of 1900. It was a good place to conduct gliding experiments because of its strong, steady wind.

The brothers made about a dozen glides, but did not have complete control of the glider. Back home they built a series of wind tunnels and experimented with miniature wings of different sizes and shapes. Eventually they replaced the tail fins with a single movable rudder to make the glider easier to control.

## First flight

Now all the brothers needed to make an airplane was an engine, but there were no engines light and powerful enough to put in an airplane. The brothers worked through most of the spring and summer of 1903 building their own engine. In September they went back to Kitty Hawk, but were delayed by engine breakdowns and bad weather.

It was not until December that the engine was in good repair and the weather was calm. On the morning of December 17, 1903, Wilbur Wright flew the plane a short distance. He was only airborne for 59 seconds, but he had made history. In 1909 the brothers formed the American Wright Company to manufacture airplanes.

Wilbur died on May 30, 1912. Orville continued to experiment and help advance the cause of aviation. He died on January 30, 1948, having lived long enough to know that a plane could fly faster than the speed of sound.

**SEE ALSO:** Aircraft; Balloon & Airship; Inventors & Inventions

# ✳ WRITERS, AMERICAN
**The stories and culture of Native Americans were passed down by word of mouth. This meant that the first American writers were Europeans.**

Much of the earliest writing from America consists of diaries and sermons by colonists. These works revolve around the writers' relationship with God. The colonies' first printing press was set up at Harvard College, Massachusetts, in 1639.

The first American writer to achieve international fame was Benjamin Franklin. His *Poor Richard's Almanack* (1733–38) became hugely popular. In 1828 Noah Webster's *An American Dictionary of the English Language* identified a specifically American language that was developing apart from the English spoken in Britain.

## American fiction
In the early 1800s novels and stories with a specifically American flavor began to appear. In the 1820s Washington Irving wrote stories about characters such as Ichabod Crane and Rip Van Winkle that are still read today. James Fenimore Cooper's novels, such as *The Last of the Mohicans* (1826), defined the popular idea of the American frontier. Nathaniel Hawthorne's most famous work, *The Scarlet Letter* (1850), is about the Puritan colonists of Salem, Massachusetts, in the 1600s.

Later novelists wrote about the social problems of the growing nation. Harriet Beecher Stowe attacked slavery in *Uncle Tom's Cabin* (1852). Stephen Crane's works focused on war and poverty. His best-known novel is *The Red Badge of Courage* (1895).

## American poetry
Poets such as Henry Wadsworth Longfellow wrote verse about the history of America. They were popular in Europe as well as the United States. Two of the nation's greatest poets wrote in the late 1800s. Walt Whitman's work is full of passion for people working together

and appreciating nature. Emily Dickinson was much more concerned with the individual's inner thoughts, and her poems are often about death.

## The 20th century
In the 1900s many novelists concentrated on the problems of society. Sinclair Lewis attacked the self-satisfied middle classes. John Dos Passos and John Steinbeck dealt sympathetically with the problems of the poor. Richard Wright, James Baldwin, Maya Angelou, and Ralph Ellison confronted racism and brought the African American perspective to a wide readership. But other writers did not deal with society in such a straightforward way. T. S. Eliot, Ezra Pound, and Gertrude Stein were all important figures in the Modernist movement. The language and structure of their writing was new and often difficult for readers.

The second half of the century saw the United States become one of the most important political, economic, and cultural

*The novelist F. Scott Fitzgerald (1896–1940) wrote about the dark side of life in the jazz age of the 1920s. The Great Gatsby is his most famous novel.*

## MAJOR AMERICAN WRITERS

These are just a few of the many writers who have shaped American literature. There are many more.

**Irving, Washington** (1783–1859)
Short story writer, influenced by New England folklore.

**Longfellow, Henry Wadsworth** (1807–1882)
Poet, wrote *The Song Of Hiawatha* and *Paul Revere's Ride*.

**Poe, Edgar Allan** (1809–49)
Short story writer and poet, wrote tales of suspense and horror.

**Stowe, Harriet (Elizabeth) Beecher** (1811–96)
Her powerful antislavery novel *Uncle Tom's Cabin* is often said to have been one of the causes of the Civil War.

**Melville, Herman** (1819–91)
Novelist, wrote tales of the sea, famously *Moby Dick*.

**James, Henry** (1843–1916)
Novelist, wrote about the relations between American and European cultures.

**Wharton, Edith (Newbold)** (1862–1937)
Novelist, wrote about women in high society.

**Henry, O. (Porter, William Sidney)** (1862–1910)
Short story writer, noted for a surprise twist at the end of his stories.

**Frost, Robert (Lee)** (1874–1963)
Based his poems on ordinary speech and set them in New England.

**Williams, William Carlos** (1883–1963)
Poet who wrote about the American landscape and people.

**Eliot, T. S. (Thomas Stearns)** (1888–1965)
Poet and critic, an important figure in the Modernist movement.

**Hurston, Zora Neale** (1891–1960)
Novelist influenced by Southern folklore.

**Faulkner, William (Cuthbert)** (1897–1962)
Novelist and short story writer, set most of his works in Mississippi.

**Steinbeck, John (Ernst)** (1902–68)
Novelist, wrote about migrant farm workers during the Depression.

**Hughes, (James) Langston** (1902–1967)
Poet and novelist of the Harlem Renaissance, wrote about the lives of ordinary black people.

**Salinger, J. D. (Jerome David)** (1919– )
Novelist and short story writer, author of *The Catcher In The Rye*.

**Walker, Alice** (1944– )
Novelist who won the Pulitzer Prize in 1983 for *The Color Purple*.

forces in the world. Authors such as Saul Bellow, Isaac Bashevis Singer, and Toni Morrison won the Nobel Prize in literature. In the past American writers looked to Europe for inspiration. Today the works of writers such as John Updike, Joan Didion, and Thomas Pynchon influence writers around the world. Although they usually deal with life in America, their style and themes are universal.

*The poet Walt Whitman (1819–92) wrote about human relationships and nature.*

*Maya Angelou (1928– ), novelist, critic, and autobiographer who writes about African American lives.*

**SEE ALSO:** Colonial America; Dickinson, Emily; Dictionary; Franklin, Benjamin; Frontier, The American; Hemingway, Ernest; Literature; Literature, Children's; Morrison, Toni; Nobel Prize; Twain, Mark; Writers, World

# ☀ WRITERS, WORLD

**People have recorded their thoughts in permanent form for over 5,000 years. But the word "writer" is usually applied to those with a skill for language.**

People communicated and told stories well before the development of writing. Tales were passed down the generations by word of mouth. Many were myths that tried to explain the mysteries of creation or the weather.

The first examples of written language come from Sumeria (modern Iraq) in about 3500 B.C. *The Epic of Gilgamesh*, a Sumerian poem from about 2500 B.C., is one of the earliest known pieces of creative writing. Some of the stories that make up the Old Testament of the Bible also date from around this time.

The ancient Greeks and Romans wrote classical works that are still read today. The great poems of Homer and Virgil and the dramas of Sophocles and Plautus influenced many later writers. The Greek writer Aesop wrote short moral stories called fables that are still popular today. Lady Murasaki, in Japan, wrote about love and politics; Shi Nai-an, in China, wrote *The Water Margin*, tales of legendary heroes and warriors.

### Printed books

From the 1200s poets, such as Dante, Boccaccio, and Chaucer, wrote long works about religion, love, and life that are still popular. However, most people still could not read. When Johannes Gutenberg invented the printing press in the 1400s, books became cheaper and easier to produce. Gradually, more people learned to read.

At the same time, people became more interested in the world around them and in how it worked. This period is called the Renaissance.

*The French novelist and poet Victor Hugo (1802–85) wrote books such as Notre-Dame de Paris (The Hunchback of Notre Dame) that criticized social and political injustice.*

Books of nonfiction—dealing with facts, not stories or poems—were important in communicating ideas.

Until the early 1800s poetry was the most popular form of imaginative writing. Even dramatists, such as Shakespeare and Moliére, usually wrote in verse. The first great European novel was Cervantes's *Don Quixote*, published in the early 1600s. In the 1700s the English writer Henry Fielding developed the form, with books such as *Tom Jones*. But the greatest novelists wrote in the 1800s. They included Charles Dickens, Jane Austen, and the Brontë sisters in England; Victor Hugo, Honoré de Balzac, and Emile Zola in France; and Leo Tolstoy and Fyodor Dostoyevsky in Russia. They used the novel to study emotions and society.

*Charlotte Brontë and her sisters Emily and Anne in England wrote poems and short stories as well as novels. Charlotte's most famous novel, Jane Eyre, is based on her experiences as a governess in a large house.*

## GREAT WRITERS

These are just a few of the world's most famous writers. There are many, many more.

**Homer** (about 800s B.C.)
Ancient Greek poet, wrote the *Iliad* and the *Odyssey*, epic (heroic) poems about the Trojan War and Odysseus's travels afterward.

**Lady Murasaki (Murasaki Shikibu)** (about A.D. 978–1026)
Japanese author and diarist, wrote the six-part *Tale of Genji*, regarded by many as the first novel.

**Dante (Alighieri)** (1265–1321)
Italian poet, wrote *The Divine Comedy*, the tale of a journey from hell to heaven.

**Chaucer, Geoffrey** (about 1343–1400)
English poet (pictured below), wrote *The Canterbury Tales*, a collection of stories told by a group of pilgrims.

**Cervantes, Miguel de** (1547–1616)
Spanish author of *Don Quixote*, an important early novel about a deluded, romantic knight.

**Milton, John** (1608–1674)
English poet, wrote *Paradise Lost*, based on the biblical stories of Adam, Eve, and Satan.

**Goethe, Johann Wolfgang von** (1749–1832)
German poet, dramatist, and novelist, wrote *Faust*, the best-known version of a legend about a scholar who sells his soul to Satan.

**Brontë, Charlotte** (1816–55), **Emily (Jane)** (1818–48), and **Anne** (1820–49)
English sisters who wrote passionate novels with strong female characters. The best known are Charlotte's *Jane Eyre* and Emily's *Wuthering Heights*.

**Eliot, George (Evans, Mary Ann)** (1819–80)
English novelist who wrote under a man's name. Her most famous work is *Middlemarch*.

**Tolstoy, Leo** (1828–1910)
Russian novelist, wrote *War and Peace* and *Anna Karenina*. A major writer about people's place in history and society.

**Woolf, (Adeline) Virginia** (1882–1941)
English novelist and essayist. Developed new, nonrealistic styles of writing fiction, particularly stream of consciousness, which mimics the flow of thoughts by using words without punctuation.

**García Márquez, Gabriel** (1928– )
Colombian novelist, wrote *One Hundred Years of Solitude*, the magical tale of an imaginary South American community.

▶ *A 19th-century illustration from the Tale of Genji by Lady Murasaki. The novel describes Japanese court society. Lady Murasaki was a lady-in-waiting at the royal court at the beginning of the 11th century.*

### Modern writers

In the 1900s some writers became dissatisfied with traditional forms of fiction and poetry. Writers such as James Joyce and Virginia Woolf were important figures in a movement called Modernism. At first many people did not understand their works because they did not always follow normal rules of grammar and sentence structure. Their books challenged traditional ideas and certainties about religion and society.

Other novelists experimented with new subjects. The French novelist Marcel Proust explored the workings of human memory and emotions in *Remembrance of Things Past*. Austrian writer Franz Kafka portrayed a frightening world of isolation and despair. German writer Thomas Mann described the conflicts between artists and society.

From the late 1900s movies, pop music, and other new art forms influenced many writers. But the most popular writers remain those who can tell a story that holds the attention—just like the storytellers who passed their tales down even before writing was invented.

**SEE ALSO:** Ancient Civilizations; Bible; Dickens, Charles; Literature; Literature, Children's; Myth & Legend; Printing; Renaissance; Shakespeare, William; Theater; Writers, American

# ✳ WRITING

**Writing is the ability to convey information, ideas, and experiences to other people in a physical form. People use writing in many different ways.**

A quick e-mail to a friend is different from an assignment for a teacher. Writing a short report for a newspaper requires different skills from writing a novel. For some people writing is a hobby, and for others it is a profession.

### Learning to write

Most writers say that they did not learn to write by following a set of rules or formulas but by practicing writing. Each writer has his or her own approach to developing a piece of writing from idea to finished piece, but the common elements in the writing process are finding an idea, drafting, revising, and copyediting.

The first decision a writer has to make is what to say. This is the initial idea or thought. Writers often carry a notebook to jot down ideas or thoughts. They may be based on the senses of sight, smell, touch, and taste, or on feelings, emotions, and reactions to a situation.

The next stage is to gather information about the subject. Writers use a variety of sources for their raw material, depending on the purpose of the writing. Libraries supply books, articles, and news clippings. Some writers also create their own reference library of magazines and relevant newspaper articles. Movies, paintings, news programs, or videos might provide information. Another source of information is to talk to people who are experts in their field, such as scientists, or those who have first-hand experience of the topic the writer has chosen.

After gathering information, the writer plans the piece of work. Most pieces of writing should have an introduction explaining the purpose of the work, a middle section where a logical argument or storyline is developed, and a conclusion summarizing the piece of work.

The next step is a first draft. This is where the writer experiments to see how the ideas work together on paper. The first draft is usually produced on a computer rather than handwritten, which makes it easier to change and correct the document. There may be several versions, or drafts, at this stage.

Writers constantly revise their work and check it for accuracy. They may also ask another person to read it and make suggestions about how it can be improved. The final stage is copyediting, when the writer checks that the spelling, grammar, and punctuation are correct.

▲
*Learning to write at school is just the beginning. Even people who are not professional writers use writing in their everyday lives—for example, writing essays, reports, records of meetings, and letters, or keeping a diary for personal satisfaction.*

**SEE ALSO:** Book Report; Dictionary; Grammar; Library; Note Taking; Punctuation; Research; Revision

# ✳ WYOMING

Wyoming is one of the Rocky Mountain states. It is one of the few states that has no boundary lines formed by mountains, rivers, or ocean shores.

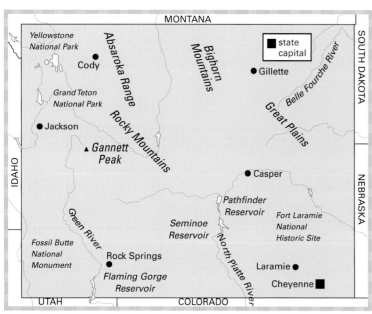

**Wyoming's state flag**

▷ *A bighorn sheep in Yellowstone National Park. Yellowstone is the nation's oldest and largest national park, and is home to a variety of wildlife.*

There are two geographical regions in Wyoming: the Great Plains and the Rocky Mountains. The Great Plains in eastern Wyoming are vast, gently rolling flats occasionally interrupted by low, steep hills. The northern part of the region contains a small part of the Black Hills, which lie mostly in South Dakota. Nearby are isolated flat-topped hills called buttes that have been eroded into unusual shapes. The most famous of them is Devils Tower, the first natural landmark to be made a national monument.

The southern part of the Great Plains contains Goshen Hole, where the valley of the North Platte River widens. Wind and water have carved the land surface, leaving a rough and broken landscape.

The Rocky Mountain region is made up of the Southern Rockies, the Middle Rockies, and the Wyoming Basin. In the northwest of the Middle Rockies is the Yellowstone Plateau, a volcanic area surrounded by lofty mountains and cut by deep, narrow valleys. To the east of the Yellowstone Plateau two massive

mountain ranges, the Absaroka Range and the Bighorn Mountains, flank the broad Bighorn Basin.

The majestic Wind River Range and Teton Mountains lie to the south of the Yellowstone Plateau. In the Tetons glaciers (rivers of ice) have carved out spectacular crags and peaks. Jackson Hole, a beautiful, fertile valley, lies at the base of this range.

The Wyoming Basin separates the Middle Rockies from the Southern Rockies. It is a vast, dry plateau with occasional low mountains, buttes, and belts of sand dunes.

In low-lying areas July temperatures average 75°F (24°C). The mountains and higher valleys are much cooler. Winter in the mountains is long and cold—annual snowfall can be more than 200 in. (5,100mm). Annual rainfall ranges from less than 6 in. (150mm) in the lower parts of the Big Horn Basin to 30 in. (750mm) at the southern entrance to Yellowstone National Park. Plain and basin areas are generally dry.

## Plant and animal life

About one-sixth of Wyoming is covered with forests, mostly within national parks. The main commercial trees are lodgepole pine and yellow pine. Yellowstone National Park is home to bears, elk, moose, bison, deer, antelope, coyotes, and Rocky Mountain sheep, as well as rare birds such as the trumpeter swan. Areas in and around Grand Teton National Park shelter a similar variety of wildlife. The National Elk Refuge near Jackson is the winter home of a large elk herd. Other elk herds are found throughout the mountainous regions of the state. Bald eagles and golden eagles nest in the state.

## People, economy, and history

People lived in Wyoming over 10,000 years ago. Later Native American peoples included the Arapaho, Crow, Sioux, Cheyenne, and Shoshone.

The first fur trappers arrived from other parts of the country in the early 1800s. Between 1842 and the 1860s many people traveled through Wyoming on their way to Oregon, Utah, or California. The main stagecoach route west crossed southern Wyoming in the 1860s.

After gold was discovered in Montana in the 1860s, the Army built forts in Wyoming. There were conflicts between the Army and Native Americans in the 1860s and 1870s.

In 1868 the Wyoming Territory was formed. Between 1870 and 1900 the population of Wyoming increased from about 9,000 to more than 90,000. This was due to the construction of the first transcontinental railroad. Coal mines were opened to supply fuel for the locomotives, and the mines hired increasing numbers of European immigrants. In 1890 Wyoming became a state.

Within ten years sheep raising had become an important industry, despite resistance from cattle ranchers. Cowboys occasionally raided sheep camps, killing sheep and terrorizing the sheepherders.

Minerals, particularly uranium, have traditionally supplied most of Wyoming's wealth. The state leads the nation in coal production. It is also the world's largest producer of sodium carbonate, which is used in making soaps, chemicals, and many other products. Tourism and agriculture are important to the economy. Wyoming's scenery and national parks attract millions of visitors each year.

**SEE ALSO:** Cowboy; Glacier; National Parks

### KEY FACTS

**AREA**
97,818 sq. mi. (253,349 sq. km); rank, 9th

**POPULATION**
493,782 (2000 census); rank, 50th

**ELEVATION**
Highest—13,804 ft. (4,207m) at Gannett Peak; lowest—3,100 ft. (945m) at Belle Fourche Creek in Crook County

**CAPITAL**
Cheyenne

**STATEHOOD**
July 10, 1890; 44th state

**ABBREVIATION**
WY

**STATE MOTTO**
Equal Rights

**STATE SONG**
"Wyoming"

**STATE NICKNAME**
Equality State

**STATE FLOWER**
Indian paintbrush

**STATE TREE**
Cottonwood

**STATE BIRD**
Western meadowlark

*Many of the peaks in Grand Teton National Park rise to 12,000 feet (3,660m). The park contains most of the Teton Mountain Range and part of the Jackson Hole high mountain valley.*

## ✳ X-RAY
**X-rays are similar to light in many ways. But there is one important difference—x-rays can penetrate many materials that will stop most forms of light.**

X-rays are beamed through an object to a sheet of photographic film. The image of the inner structure of the object is recorded on the film. The material in one part of the object may be penetrated by many more x-rays than the material in another part. This difference will show on the film, revealing the inner structure of the object. One use of x-rays is to inspect machinery and metal parts for flaws.

### Medical uses
Doctors use x-rays to show the inner parts of the body. X-rays can tell the difference between bone, soft tissues (muscles, blood vessels, and major organs), fat, and air (in the lungs). An x-ray picture of an arm shows the bones because the x-rays cannot move through them as easily as the muscles around them. A chest x-ray shows the heart surrounded by air in the lungs. The branch of medicine that uses x-rays is called radiology.

In the late 1960s scientists developed an x-ray machine called a computerized axial tomography (CAT) scanner. It is a combination of an x-ray machine and a computer. The CAT scanner produces cross-sectional views of the body and is particularly useful for examining the brain, chest, and stomach.

### History
X-rays were discovered accidentally by the German scientist Wilhelm Conrad Roentgen in 1895, when he was experimenting with a special kind of lamp called a cathode-ray tube. Although Roentgen learned how to produce the new rays and became familiar with their characteristics, he never found out exactly what they were. For this reason he called them x-rays, "x" standing for unknown.

**SEE ALSO:** Light; Medicine; Scientific Instruments; Scientist

### HOW X-RAYS WORK

▶ *The best-known use of x-rays is in medicine. The beam of x-rays is sent through the patient's body onto a plate of photographic film. Bones absorb a large amount of the x-rays and show up as white shadows on the film. Other tissues absorb fewer x-rays, so they show up as gray areas.*

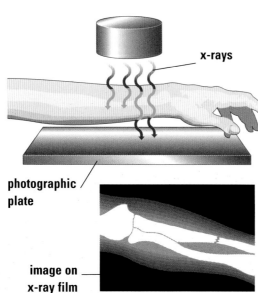

x-rays

photographic plate

image on x-ray film

# Y

*YEMEN **see** *MIDDLE EAST

*YUGOSLAVIA **see** *BALKANS

## *YUKON TERRITORY

The Yukon Territory lies in the northwestern corner of Canada's mainland. It borders British Columbia, Alaska, Northwest Territories, and the Beaufort Sea.

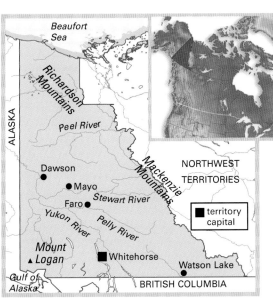

Most of the Yukon consists of a high central plateau—about 3,940 ft. (1,200m) above sea level—broken up by mountains and deep valleys. Many of the Yukon's mountains are covered by permanent ice caps. They include Canada's tallest peaks—Mount Logan is the highest mountain in Canada.

Winters are mostly very cold. The lowest temperature ever recorded in Canada is –81°F (–63°C) at Snag. Summers are warm and can be hot.

### Plant and animal life
Much of the Yukon's forest is very sparse and slow growing. Fish, bears, and caribou are traditionally important for food and clothing.

### People, history, and economy
Native Americans and Inuits have

**Yukon territory flag**

lived in the area for centuries, and Native Americans now make up about 20 percent of the population. Over 75 percent of the population live in the Whitehorse area. In 1896 gold was discovered at Bonanza Creek, starting the world's biggest gold rush. In 1898 the Yukon became a separate territory.

Although there are still gold, silver, zinc, lead, and copper mines, the mining industry began to decline in the late 20th century. The population is also decreasing. Today tourism and government provide the majority of jobs.

SEE ALSO: Canada; Inuit

## KEY FACTS

**AREA**
205,346 sq. mi. (531,844 sq. km); rank, 3rd territory

**POPULATION**
29,900 (2001 census); rank, 2nd territory

**ELEVATION**
Highest—19,524 ft. (5,951m) at Mt. Logan; lowest—sea level

**CAPITAL**
Whitehorse

**TERRITORY ESTABLISHED**
1898

**TERRITORY MOTTO**
No official motto

**TERRITORY FLOWER**
Purple firewood

**TERRITORY TREE**
Subalpine fir

**TERRITORY BIRD**
Common raven

*ZAMBIA ⟨see⟩ *AFRICA, SOUTHERN

*ZIMBABWE ⟨see⟩ *AFRICA, SOUTHERN

# *ZOOLOGY

Zoology is the branch of science that deals with all aspects of animal life. The word comes from the Greek for "knowledge of animals."

*A zoologist tags a loggerhead turtle at the Archie Carr National Wildlife Refuge in Florida, where the habitat and nesting areas of the turtles are being protected.*

Scientists studied animals thousands of years ago. Aristotle, in ancient Greece, and Pliny the Elder, in Rome, both tried to classify all animal species.

In the 1500s Leonardo da Vinci and Andreas Vesalius dissected (cut up) animals in order to discover more about the body. In the 1700s Carolus Linnaeus created the modern system of classifying animals. It uses a different Latin name for each kind of animal.

In the 1800s the English scientist Charles Darwin was the first to publish a theory of evolution—that animal species adapt to their environments over generations. The 1900s saw new discoveries about inheritance involving genes and DNA. These developments expanded scientific knowledge about all forms of life, including animals. In recent years zoologists have taken a more active role in protecting animal life, not just observing but campaigning against human activity that puts animals in danger.

Some zoologists concentrate on observing animals in their natural habitat. They may be researching animal behavior or seeking ways to protect endangered species. Others work in zoos or safari parks. Many species of animal would now be extinct (died out) if they had not been kept in captivity. Zoologists working in natural history museums also use their knowledge to inform the public.

Many zoologists work in universities or laboratories. They study live animals and cell samples. Their scientific discoveries benefit humans as well as animals.

SEE ALSO: Animal; Aristotle; Biology; Botany; DNA; Environment; Evolution; Genetics; Leonardo da Vinci; Science; Scientist

# ✻ SET INDEX

Numbers in **bold type** are
volume numbers. Page
numbers in *italics* refer to
pictures or their captions.

## PICTURE CREDITS

l = left  r = right,  t = top  c = center  b = bottom  ba = background

**AKG London:** 15t; **Art Explosion:** 15b; **Corbis:** Bass Museum of Art 48t, Bettmann 30t, 44, 46b, First Light 18, Araldo da Luca 14, Richard T. Nowitz 28, Craig Tuttle 17; **Digital Vision:** 21, 31; **Getty Images:** Archive Photos 7t, 8, /Joe Munroe 43, /Nickolas Murray/George Eastman House 45; **Hemera Digital Technologies Inc.:** 24b; **John Foxx Images & Images 4 Communication:** 19, 49; **Library of Congress Prints & Photographs Division:** (repro.no. LC-USZ62-13227) 25, (repro.no.LC-USZ62-2226DLC) 35, (repro.no.LC-USZ62-30776) 36, (repro.no.LC-USZ62-82799) 46t; **Mary Evans Picture Library:** 9, 34, 47; **National Archives and Records Administration:** 20, 30b, 38, 39, 41b; **NASA:** JPL 3; **Nature Picture Library:** Premaphoto 42; **NHPA:** John Shaw 4, 32; **Photodisc:** 37, PhotoLink/C. Solum 51, Stock Trek 16t; **Photos12.com:** ARJ 24t; **Rex Features Ltd:** John Hannah 16b; **Robert Hunt Library:** 26, 40, 41t, **South American Pictures:** Chris Sharp 22; **Still Pictures:** Mark Edwards 23; **Topham:** 48b, 7b; The British Museum/HIP 11; The Image Works 27; **U.S. Fish & Wildlife Service:** John & Karen Hollingsworth 54; **U.S. Geological Survey:** 13; **U.S. Department of Agriculture:** Ron Nichols 33; **Virginia Tourism Coporation:** 12; **Wyoming Travel and Tourism:** 50 **Cover: Digital Vision** ba; **NASA:** JPL l; **Robert Hunt Library** c; **National Archives and Records Administration** r.